SON OF ORIGINS OF MARVEL COMICS

Revised Edition

STAN LEE

SON OF ORIGINS OF MARVEL COMICS™ Revised Edition

Contains material originally published in Sons of Origins of Marvel Comics, Vol. 1. Published by MARVEL COMICS; 387 PARK AVENUE SOUTH, NEW YORK, N.Y. 10016. Copyright © 1975, 1997 Marvel Characters, Inc.
Printed in the U.S.A. First Printing, November, 1997.

ISBN #0-7851-0559-X. GST #R127032852.

*To the mighty Marvel Bullpen—chaotic, capricious,
charismatic, confused . . . and still the most titanically
talented aggregation of storytellers, both visual
and verbal, ever to come down the pike*

TABLE OF CONTENTS

INTRODUCTIONS BY STAN LEE

Chapter 1

by Stan Lee, Jack Kirby, Paul Reinman, Chris Claremont,

Jim Lee and Scott Williams

Chapter 2

by Stan Lee, Larry Lieber, Don Heck, David Michelinie,

Mark Bright, and Bob Layton

Chapter 3

by Stan Lee, Jack Kirby, Bob Harras,

Steve Epting and Tom Palmer

Chapter 4

by Stan Lee, Bill Everett,

Frank Miller and David Mazzucchelli

Chapter 5

by Stan Lee, John Buscema, and Joe Sinnott.

(special thanks to Roger Bonas and Repro, and Eric Fein)

PROLOGUE

Welcome back, O Seeker of the Truth.

No sooner did our first frenetic volume, *Origins of Marvel Comics*, lavish a cornucopia of culture upon a grateful human race than we were immediately besieged with requests for an equally illuminating sequel. Touched by your entreaties, warmed by your enthusiasm, and spurred by our own gnawing greed, we herewith present the second stellar production in a series that threatens to go on forever. But, before you breathlessly partake of the wonderment that awaits you, let us pause for a moment to rapturously recapture the essence of our previous tome.

As you may recall, the Marvel Comics Group first burst upon the public consciousness with Issue #1 of *The Fantastic Four* in the year 1961. The ol' FF, as it soon became known by the comicbook cognoscenti, heralded a new style of costumed superheroes—more realistic, truer-to-life adventurers, heroes plagued with the problems that torment us all: money worries, romantic hangups, feelings of inadequacy, jealousy, vanity, and fear. In fact, the FF were so vulnerable, so fallible, so typically human in their moods and reactions that they became overnight favorites throughout the length and breadth of superhero fandom. Within the very first few issues, *The Fantastic Four* could lay claim to being one of the world's best-selling comicbooks, and it's still king of the castle today.

A short time later Marvel introduced its second offbeat original in the person of The Incredible Hulk. Victim of a gamma-ray accident which had transformed him from the brilliant Dr. Bruce Banner to a green-skinned monster, The Hulk could hardly be considered a typical comicbook hero. Yet, despite his outrageousness, or perhaps because of it, our jolly green giant soon followed the FF right to the top of the bestseller list and into the hearts of the fans.

By now we were flushed with success and drunk with power. Once again we recklessly flew in the face of all established tradition and dared to create a hero out of a shy, studious, insecure, mollycoddled momma's boy—or, to be more precise, an aunt's nephew. Naturally, we're referring to the first, unforgettable appearance of the amazing Spider-Man, the world-famous wall-crawler who has since become the most popular superhero in all of comicdom.

The final portions of our previous volume allowed you to witness the creation of two additional Marvel masterworks, the mighty Thor, God of Thunder, and Dr. Strange, Master of the Mystic Arts. Both the theurgical Thunder God with his double existence on Asgard and Earth, and the thaumaturgic doctor with his sorcery and spells soon joined our other dazzling do-gooders to comprise the first five luminaries in Marvel's ever-growing galaxy of superhero stars.

But, as all True Believers know so well, our first fabulous creations were but the beginning, merely the tip of a towering iceberg of ideas. Within the onrushing weeks and months that followed, new heroes, new villains, new titles were created with breathtaking speed. Marvel had just begun to grow, and the end was nowhere in sight.

This then is a not-too-critical chronicle of the mighty strips that followed, and of the new, sensational characters who have themselves become legends within their own time.

And now, read on. The best lies just ahead.

PART ONE

MAKE WAY FOR THE MERRY MUTANTS

THE YEAR 1963 was a bounteous bonanza for superheroes. At Marvel Comics we were grinding them out like popcorn, and they seemed to be just as habit-forming.

Now, since we have to start somewhere, let's zero in on the creation of one of the most oddball teams of costumed cavorters to make their debut that year, or any other year. In the riotous realm of superherodom, they're not exactly what you'd call a typical group of gregarious grapplers, but then Marvel has never quite been known for being overly typical.

It all started when Jolly Jack Kirby and I were scrounging around for a dynamite new feature to inflict upon the hapless hordes of fandom. For those of you who may have been injudicious enough not to have read our preceding volume, let me explain that Jolly Jack was our numero uno when it came to illustrating superhero strips. Jack was (and still is) to superheroes what Kellogg's is to corn flakes. When such fabulous features as The Fantastic Four, the Mighty Thor, and The Incredible Hulk were just a-borning, it was good ol' Jackson with whom I huddled, harangued, and hassled until the characters were designed, the plots were delineated, and the layouts were delivered so that I could add the little dialogue balloons and captions with which I've spent a lifetime cluttering up the illustrations of countless long-suffering artists.

At any rate, I was anxious to come up with a new concept, and there was a germ of an idea buzzing around my head. Almost all of our heroes had gotten their superpowers from some outside source. Spider-Man had been bitten by a radioactive spider (could happen to anyone); the Hulk had been the victim of a gamma-ray explosion; with The Fantastic Four it was a sudden prolonged dose of cosmic rays; and, just to show we weren't getting into a rut, Thor had gained his godlike power by picking up a rough wooden cane inside a mysterious cave.

Of course, it's hard to remember that far back, but I suspect that I was beginning to fear our readers might get the idea we were implying that gaining a superpower was as easy as getting an insect bite, being in the vicinity of a gamma or cosmic ray, or picking up a stick.

'Twas time for a new approach—and I thought I had the angle.

Why not create a group of characters who were born with their unique abilities? Why not offer the reader a protagonist who was not dependent upon some far-fetched pseudo-scientific accident? But, if a character has a superpower (and superpowers are the name of the game in the madcap world of Marvel) and if no explanation is given, how do we make that character's attributes acceptable to our finicky far-flung audience? There was only one possible answer—we would create a team of mutants!

Mutant! One who undergoes a hypothetical unexpected change in heredity, producing a new individual who is basically unlike the parent. Or, to put it more succinctly, a freak, an aberration of nature— one who has been changed for the better, or the worse.

The minute it hit me I knew the concept was basically sound. Mutation is a scientific fact of life; it's plausible, possible, practical, and provable. Best of all, it would allow Jack and me the fullest scope for our imaginations. When thinking of all possible variations of normal human beings, the sky's the limit—whatever power we conceived of could be justified on the basis of its being a mutated trait.

No sooner did I discuss the basic premise with Jack than we were off and running. We decided to create two groups of mutants, one evil and the other good. One would be eternally striving to subjugate mankind, and the other would be ceaselessly battling to protect the human race. The more we discussed it, the better I liked it. One of the biggest problems in the comicbook field is the difficulty of finding new storylines which don't seem to be bland imitations of the thousands of stories that have gone before. It's a mind-boggling task to be compelled to come up with dozens of new heroes and villains regularly, and still to give them an air of freshness and surprise. But this time it seemed we had a ready-made vehicle, something refreshingly new and totally different.

Let me digress long enough to mention another problem that always crops up in the development of any new strip—the problem of the title. This time I thought we had it made. There was one logical, obvious, perfect title for such a feature. It would look dramatic upon the front cover of the magazine, it had a perfect ring to it, it would be easy to letter and easier to remember. Our strip would be about a group of mutants, right? Their power would be a mutant power, right? The good guys would be mutants and the bad guys would be mutants, right? Okay then, nothing could be more natural than to call the book *The Mutants,* right? Guess again, Charlie!

And now, we have to backtrack a bit for a better understanding of what I'm talking about. At the time in question, back in 1963, I was editor, art director, and head writer of Marvel Comics. Although the comicbooks were my responsibility, and basically my babies, I was answerable to the publisher who employed me, a stalwart by the name of Martin Goodman. Although Martin and I saw eye-to-eye on most editorial matters, there was one area in which we were worlds apart. To him, comics were primarily written and drawn for little kids, and he was always afraid of anything going into the magazines which might be over their heads. To me, there was a whole world of older readers just waiting to be tapped, and I felt they could be reached without our losing any of the bubble-gum brigade. I was certain that younger kids are a lot smarter and more knowledgeable than was generally supposed, and they'd have no difficulty following and enjoying any of our stories which might be slanted to the older reader. Actually, that point has been fairly well proven in the past few years, since I've become publisher of Marvel. By telling our tales on two levels—color, costumes, and exaggerated action for the kids; science-fiction, satire, and sophisticated philosophy for the adults and near-adults—we've managed to expand the perimeters of our audience to the point where we presently have as many readers from the ages of 15 to 25 as we have from 6 to 15. In fact, one of the most gratifying successes we've enjoyed has been in the area of vocabulary. The language employed in most of the Marvel Comics publications is generally of college level, and, judging by our sales figures, surveys, and our continual avalanche of fan mail, we haven't lost a single youthful reader due to his being exposed to a mature and intelligent presentation of the English language.

At any rate, Martin felt the title *The Mutants* would be too difficult for little kids to understand. He felt they wouldn't know what the word "mutant" meant. When I suggested that they could ask a friend, or look it up in the dictionary, he took a somewhat less than charitable view of my well-meaning proposal. Anyway, since he was the boss, the world of literature was destined to be tragically deprived of *The Mutants* as a Marvel title in the fateful year 1963.

A most apt and accurate axiom in the field of comics is the fact that without a title there can be no book. The die was cast—the gauntlet flung! We had a concept. We had a storyline. For want of a title we would not forsake our brainchild! After hours of head-scratching, soul-searching, breast-beating, and nit-picking I finally had it. Mutants have an extra power, extra ability, some extra facet or quality denied a normal man. The word "extra" was the key. Mutants are, in a sense, people with something extra. And, if we think of the word "extra" in phonetic terms, we might think of that phrase as "people with something x-tra." And a man with something x-tra could conceivably be called an x-man! Therefore, since we were discussing a whole group of mutants, why not call the book *The X-Men*? (Especially since women's lib wasn't an issue in those days, and nobody would fault us for the fact that we were callously ignoring the female member of the team—unintentionally, to be sure.) Even our peerless publisher couldn't claim that the youngest reader would have difficulty recognizing the letter "x," and the word "x-men" did have a juicy, mysterious ring to it; so we had our title, and a comicbook was born.

Then the fun really began. By far the most satisfying task in producing a superhero strip (or any form of story) is the creation and development of the various characters. And what an awesome array we had to work with! My own personal favorite was the crippled Professor Xavier, better known of course as Professor X. Next, I sort of cottoned to the brooding Cyclops, who was destined to become leader of the team after many subsequent issues. After a while I felt The Beast was too similar to The Thing (from *The Fantastic Four*), and in the issues that followed I changed his manner of speech completely, making him the most verbose, articulate, and eloquent of the group. The Angel's wings fascinated me, especially the way Jack created a harness to hold them back under his jacket when he was dressed in street clothes, and, while I got a kick out of Iceman's unique mutant power, it was Marvel Girl's spirit and total unflappability that really turned me on. As for our quintessential villain, I have always felt that Magneto represented one of the most sinister and fascinating super-foes we've ever concocted. The helmet that Jack fashioned for him was a sheer masterpiece, and I've never been able to figure out exactly how old he is behind those crazy metal blinders.

But now it's time to turn you loose in the "danger room" of a strange, isolated old mansion, where you can relive once again the original, unforgettable experience of discovering the strangest super-heroes of all!

IN THE MAIN STUDY OF AN EXCLUSIVE PRIVATE SCHOOL IN NEW YORK'S WESTCHESTER COUNTY, A STRANGE SILENT MAN SITS MOTIONLESS, BROODING... ALONE WITH HIS INDESCRIBABLE THOUGHTS...

FINALLY, HIS MEDITATION COMES TO AN END! THEN, WHILE HE REMAINS COMPLETELY MOTIONLESS, A SHARP, COMMANDING THOUGHT RINGS OUT, ECHOING THROUGH THE GREAT HALLS OF THE BUILDING!

ATTENTION, X-MEN! THIS IS PROFESSOR XAVIER CALLING! REPEAT: THIS IS PROFESSOR X CALLING!

YOU ARE ORDERED TO APPEAR AT ONCE! CLASS IS NOW IN SESSION! TARDINESS WILL BE PUNISHED!

NEVER, WITHIN THE MEMORY OF MAN, WAS THERE A "CLASS" SUCH AS THIS! NEVER WAS THERE A "TEACHER" SUCH AS PROFESSOR X! AND NEVER WERE THERE "STUDENTS" SUCH AS THE...

"X-MEN"

CYCLOPS PRESENT AND ACCOUNTED FOR, SIR!

THE ANGEL REPORTING, SIR!

ICEMAN RIGHT ON SCHEDULE, SIR!

THE BEAST IS HERE, SIR!

Written by:
STAN LEE
Drawn by:
JACK KIRBY
Inked by:
PAUL REINMAN
Lettered by:
S. ROSEN

K-401

AND NOW, PREPARE YOURSELF FOR ONE OF THE MOST EXCITING READING EXPERIENCES OF YOUR LIFE! FOR YOU ARE ABOUT TO ENTER THE FASCINATING, UNPREDICTABLE WORLD OF... THE X-MEN!

15

EXCELLENT! NOW SPIN AROUND! FASTER! FASTER! PRETEND AN ENEMY IS SHOOTING AT YOU! YOU MUST MAKE YOURSELF AN IMPOSSIBLE TARGET!

AND NOW, AT MY COMMAND, RELEASE YOURSELF FROM THE TAUT WIRE AND EXECUTE MANEUVER "G"! YOU HAVE EXACTLY THREE SECONDS!

GO!

THREE SECONDS EXACTLY! WELL DONE, BEAST!

NOW FOR YOUR BALANCE DRILL! STEADY... STEADY! SLACKEN THE TENSION, CYCLOPS!

GOOD!! NOW, AS THE ROD BEGINS TO SAG, MAINTAIN YOUR BALANCE... ON ONE FINGER! HOLD IT! HOLD IT!

TOO FAST! YOU'RE SWAYING TOO MUCH! RECOVER... QUICKLY! NOW LAND ON YOUR FEET BEFORE THE ROD SNAPS BACK! CAREFUL... CAREFUL...

WHEW... HOW'D I DO, SIR?

YOU'LL RECEIVE YOUR GRADE TOMORROW! ALL RIGHT, ANGEL... IT'S YOUR TURN!

ARE YOU RECEIVING MY THOUGHT CLEARLY? GOOD! NOW, BE SHARP... TODAY WE TEST YOUR WING REFLEX! YOU DARE NOT MAKE A MISTAKE!

MISTAKES ARE FOR HOMO SAPIENS, SIR... NOT THE ANGEL!

18

19

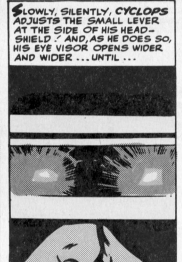

HEY!! THAT'S NOT *FAIR!* YOU'RE OPENIN' THAT COTTON-PICKIN' *VISOR* OF YOURS *WIDER!*

ICEMAN, FOR THE KIND OF CAREER *WE'RE* TRAINING FOR, THERE'S NO SUCH WORD AS "FAIR"!

NOW *PROTECT YOURSELF!* MY ENERGY BEAM IS SMASHING THROUGH!

THIS IS *ONE* DAY I SHOULDA STOOD IN BED!

OKAY... TURN THAT BLAMED BEAM *OFF,* WILLYA?

ANGEL! BEAST! JOIN ICEMAN! TRY TO SUBDUE CYCLOPS!

WHUP

THANKS, PROF! I COULD *USE* A LITTLE HELP!

IT IS NOT FOR YOUR SAKE ALONE, LAD! A FEW MINUTES OF ROUGH-HOUSE IS GOOD FOR *ALL* OF YOU...TO HELP YOU LET OFF STEAM!

THEN, SUDDENLY, MINUTES LATER, A SHARP COMMANDING THOUGHT PIERCES THE BRAIN OF EACH OF THE FOUR RAMPAGING YOUTHS...

ENOUGH! THE LESSON IS OVER! WE MUST TURN OUR ENERGIES TO *DIFFERENT* MATTERS! RETURN TO YOUR PLACES... *AT ONCE!!*

STUNNED BY THE FORCE AND EXPLOSIVE POWER OF *PROFESSOR XAVIER'S* MENTAL COMMAND, THE *X-MEN* RECOIL AND DRAW BACK, THEIR FRIENDLY FREE-FOR-ALL COMPLETELY FORGOTTEN!

WHEW! HE ALMOST BOWLED ME OVER WITH *THAT* ONE!

LET'S SIMMER DOWN AND SEE WHAT HAPPENS NEXT!

I CONGRATULATE YOU ALL! YOU HAVE MASTERED READING MY THOUGHTS PERFECTLY! AND NOW I SHALL RETURN TO NORMAL SPEECH COMMUNICATION!

YOU MAY BE INTERESTED TO LEARN THAT AT THIS VERY MOMENT I SENSE A TAXI APPROACHING OUR MAIN GATE! WITHIN THAT VEHICLE IS A NEW PUPIL....A MOST ATTRACTIVE *YOUNG LADY!*

7.

YOU'RE RIGHT, SIR! WOW! SHE'S A REAL LIVING DOLL!

A REDHEAD! LOOK AT THAT FACE...AND THE REST OF HER!

ALL OF A SUDDEN, I'M IN NO HURRY TO GRADUATE FROM THIS PLACE!

A GIRL...BIG DEAL! I'M GLAD I'M NOT A WOLF LIKE YOU GUYS!

I'M GLAD, TOO! WHO NEEDS THE EXTRA COMPETITION FROM ICEMAN?!

I WONDER WHAT SUPER-HUMAN POWERS SHE POSSESSES! SHE LOOKS NORMAL ENOUGH!

WELL, LET'S GO IN AND CHANGE, SO WE DON'T SCARE HER WHEN SHE FIRST SEES US!

COME IN, MY CHILD! I AM PROFESSOR XAVIER! I AM GLAD YOU RECEIVED MY MESSAGE!

IT ALL SEEMED SO STRANGE, PROFESSOR, AND SO... MYSTERIOUS! I WAS TO TELL NO ONE BUT MY PARENTS THAT I'M COMING HERE... AND YOU DIDN'T DESCRIBE THE COURSE OF STUDY!

WHAT KIND OF SCHOOL IS THIS, SIR? I HAVE A RIGHT TO KNOW!

I THINK YOU ALREADY SUSPECT, MISS GREY! YOU SEE, I CAN READ YOUR THOUGHTS QUITE CLEARLY... AND I KNOW ALL ABOUT YOUR UNUSUAL "TALENT"!

YOU, MISS GREY, LIKE THE OTHER FOUR STUDENTS AT THIS MOST EXCLUSIVE SCHOOL, ARE A MUTANT! YOU POSSESS AN EXTRA POWER.. ONE WHICH ORDINARY HUMANS DO NOT! THAT IS WHY I CALL MY STUDENTS ... X-MEN, FOR EX-TRA POWER!

AND HERE THEY ARE NOW! ALLOW ME TO PRESENT THEM TO YOU! FROM LEFT TO RIGHT WE HAVE HANK McCOY, KNOWN TO US AS THE BEAST! BOBBY DRAKE, NICKNAMED ICEMAN! SLIM SUMMERS, OUR HUMAN CYCLOPS! AND WARREN WORTHINGTON THE THIRD, WHO IS CALLED THE ANGEL! BOYS, THIS IS MISS JEAN GREY! SHE WILL BE KNOWN AS MARVEL GIRL!

WELCOME TO THE X-MEN, MISS GREY!

THANK YOU, JEAN! AND NOW LET ME TELL YOU MORE ABOUT MY SCHOOL...

I WAS BORN OF PARENTS WHO HAD WORKED ON THE FIRST A-BOMB PROJECT! LIKE YOURSELVES, I AM A MUTANT... POSSIBLY THE FIRST SUCH MUTANT! I HAVE THE POWER TO READ MINDS, AND TO PROJECT MY OWN THOUGHTS INTO THE BRAINS OF OTHERS!

BUT, WHEN I WAS YOUNG, NORMAL PEOPLE FEARED ME, DISTRUSTED ME! I REALIZED THE HUMAN RACE IS NOT YET READY TO ACCEPT THOSE WITH EXTRA POWERS! SO I DECIDED TO BUILD A HAVEN... A SCHOOL FOR X-MEN!

HERE WE STAY, UNSUSPECTED BY NORMAL HUMANS, AS WE LEARN TO USE OUR POWERS FOR THE BENEFIT OF MANKIND... TO HELP THOSE WHO WOULD DISTRUST US IF THEY KNEW OF OUR EXISTENCE!

DUE TO A CHILDHOOD ACCIDENT, I MYSELF MUST REMAIN IN THIS CHAIR, BUT THROUGH A MASTER CONTROL PANEL I HAVE MANY DEVICES AT MY COMMAND... AND THROUGH MY MIND, I AM ALWAYS IN TOUCH WITH MY X-MEN!

AND NOW, I LEAVE YOU TO GET TO KNOW EACH OTHER BETTER!

LET ME BE THE FIRST TO WELCOME YOU TO THE X-MEN, BEAUTIFUL! MMMMM!

OH!

HANK! TAKE YOUR PAWS OFF HER!

FOR THE LUVVA PETE!

DON'T WORRY, WARREN! I'M NOT EXACTLY HELPLESS, AS YOU CAN SEE!

OH! BOY! WHAT A GAL! I HOPE SHE KEEPS THAT BIG APE UP THERE FOREVER!

HEY, C'MON! HAVE A HEART! I WAS ONLY TRYING TO BE FRIENDLY!

A FELLA COULD GET DIZZY UP HERE! LEMME DOWN, HUH? THIS IS EMBARRASSING!

VERY WELL, I'LL LET YOU DOWN!

10.

THERE! YOU'RE DOWN!

OOOFF!!

WHUMP!

I HOPE I WASN'T TOO ROUGH ON THE POOR DEAR!

NOT AT ALL, JEAN! WE DON'T USE KID GLOVES HERE! WE HAVE TO MAKE OUR TRAINING AS ROUGH AS POSSIBLE, TO PREPARE OUR-SELVES FOR OUR MISSION IN THE OUTSIDE WORLD!

THAT'S WHAT I'VE WANTED TO ASK! JUST WHAT EXACTLY IS OUR REAL MISSION, SIR?

JEAN, THERE ARE MANY MUTANTS WALK-ING THE EARTH... AND MORE ARE BORN EACH YEAR!

NOT ALL OF THEM WANT TO HELP MANKIND!... SOME HATE THE HUMAN RACE, AND WISH TO DESTROY IT! SOME FEEL THAT THE MUTANTS SHOULD BE THE REAL RULERS OF EARTH! IT IS OUR JOB TO PROTECT MANKIND FROM THOSE... FROM THE EVIL MUTANTS!

AT THAT VERY MOMENT, JUST SUCH A MUTANT PREPARES TO STRIKE... IN A SECRET LABORA-TORY NEAR CAPE CITADEL!

THE MOMENT IS AT HAND!

ALL MY MONTHS OF PREPARATION AND PLANNING SHALL NOW PAY OFF!

THE HUMAN RACE NO LONGER DESERVES DOMINION OVER THE PLANET EARTH! THE DAY OF THE MUTANTS IS UPON US

THE FIRST PHASE OF MY PLAN SHALL BE TO SHOW MY POWER...TO MAKE HOMO SAPIENS BOW TO HOMO SUPERIOR!

THE MIGHTIEST ROCKET OF ALL IS ABOUT TO BE LAUNCHED! USING MAXIMUM SECURITY PRECAUTIONS, THE GOVERNMENT FEELS NOTHING CAN PREVENT ITS SUCCESSFUL FLIGHT!

BUT HERE, MILES FROM THE LAUNCH-ING SITE, I, THE MIRACULOUS MAGNETO, ALONE SHALL MAKE A MOCKERY OF THEIR GREATEST EFFORT!

11.

25

AHHH! I CAN FEEL THE IRRESISTIBLE WAVES OF PURE MAGNETIC ENERGY SURGING FROM ME! NOW, BY EXERTING EVERY IOTA OF POWER, I CAN DIRECT THAT ENERGY UPWARD... UPWARD...

...UNTIL IT STRIKES THE SPEEDING MISSILE, CAUSING IT TO CHANGE DIRECTION...TO FALTER...TO LOSE ALTITUDE!

...TO BE COMPLETELY, IRREVOCABLY DESTROYED!!

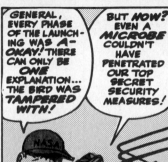

GENERAL, EVERY PHASE OF THE LAUNCHING WAS A-OKAY! THERE CAN ONLY BE ONE EXPLANATION... THE BIRD WAS TAMPERED WITH!

BUT HOW? EVEN A MICROBE COULDN'T HAVE PENETRATED OUR TOP SECRET SECURITY MEASURES!

THE NEXT DAY, THE SHOCKING NEWS IS TRANSMITTED TO A STARTLED PUBLIC...

INCREDIBLE! IT'S ALMOST AS THOUGH A DESTRUCT- IVE GHOST IS RUNNING AMOK AT THE CAPE!

EXTRA! EXTRA! ANOTHER MISSILE FAILS! EXTRA!

DAILY GLOBE FINAL

SIXTH TOP SECRET LAUNCHING FAILS AT SEA!

PHANTOM SABOTEUR STRIKES AGAIN!

BUT THE WORST IS YET TO COME! LATER THAT AFTERNOON, AT THE HEAVILY GUARDED FENCE SURROUNDING THE LAUNCHING SITE...

KEEP THAT GUN STEADY! WHY IS IT QUIVERING THAT WAY?

W-WE'RE NOT DOIN' IT, SIR! IT...IT'S MOVIN' BY ITSELF!!

12.

SUDDENLY, LIKE A LIVING THING, THE MACHINE GUN LEAPS INTO THE AIR, SPINS AROUND, AND BEGINS TO FIRE WILDLY IN ALL DIRECTIONS!

RUN FOR COVER!! THE GUN IS OUT OF CONTROL!!

BUT, THE MACHINE GUN IS NOT THE *ONLY* THING THAT SUDDENLY, MADDENINGLY SEEM TO GO AMOK!

RUN! THE TANK IS MOVING BY *ITSELF!* GANGWAY!

IT..IT'S *IMPOSSIBLE!* AND YET...IT'S ACTING LIKE IT HAS A MIND OF ITS OWN! LIKE IT'S *TRYING* TO MENACE US!

SWISH!

CLANK!

CLANK!

WITHIN SECONDS, THE ENTIRE INSTALLATION IS ALARMED, AS EMERGENCY MEASURES ARE SWIFTLY BROUGHT INTO PLAY! AND THEN...

SOUND THE ALARM! *CONDITION RED!* ALERT THE PENTAGON!

GENERAL! *LOOK!* ABOVE US...IN THE SKY!

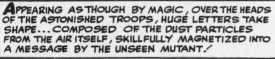

APPEARING AS THOUGH BY MAGIC, OVER THE HEADS OF THE ASTONISHED TROOPS, HUGE LETTERS TAKE SHAPE...COMPOSED OF THE DUST PARTICLES FROM THE AIR ITSELF, SKILLFULLY MAGNETIZED INTO A MESSAGE BY THE UNSEEN MUTANT!

SURRENDER THE BASE OR I'LL TAKE IT BY FORCE!

Magneto

MAGNETO? WHO...*WHAT* IS MAGNETO??

GENERAL, WHAT DOES IT *MEAN?* IS SOMEONE PLAYING A GRIM *PRANK?*

YOU SAW THAT MACHINE GUN...THAT TANK...RAMPAGING OUT OF CONTROL! THIS IS *NO JOKE,* COLONEL!

THEY ARE STARTLED! *GOOD!* THE ELEMENT OF SURPRISE IS IN MY FAVOR!

BUT THEY'RE MAKING NO MOVE TO SURRENDER! PERHAPS THEY NEED *ANOTHER* DEMONSTRATION OF MY POWER!

I'LL DIRECT MY MAGNETIC IMPULSES INTO THIS ENERGIZER, TO INCREASE THEIR POWER, AND THEN I'LL LEAVE THE HELPLESS HOMO SAPIENS WITH NO ROOM FOR DOUBT!

AN INSTANT LATER, INVISIBLE WAVES OF PURE, POWERFUL MAGNETIC ENERGY FLOW IRRESISTIBLY INTO AN UNDER-GROUND SILO WHERE ONE OF DEMOCRACY'S SILENT SENTINELS WAIT, AT THE READY!

AND THEN, MANIPULATED BY A SINISTER INTELLIGENCE, MANY HUNDREDS OF YARDS AWAY, THE MAGNETIC FORCE LIFTS THE SILO HEAD, ACTIVATING THE MIGHTY MISSILE!!

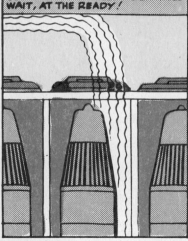

DEMONSTRATING A POWER WHICH THE HUMAN BRAIN IS ALMOST UNABLE TO COMPREHEND, MAGNETO CAUSES THE GRIM ROCKET TO FALL INTO THE SEA MANY MILES FROM SHORE, NEXT TO AN UNMANNED TARGET SHIP!

BUT STILL, THE THOUGHT OF SURRENDER NEVER CROSSES THE MINDS OF THE FIGHTING-MAD BASE PERSONNEL!

SERGEANT! ORDER THE GUARD DOUBLED AT EVERY MISSILE CONTROL CENTER! ANY ROCKET DEEMED A MENACE IS TO BE DESTROYED INSTANTLY!

SOME POWER BEYOND OUR UNDERSTANDING IS AFFECTING OUR WEAPONS! WE MUST FIND THIS MAGNETO!

GENERAL, LOOK! THAT COMMOTION AT THE MAIN GATE! IT SEEMS THAT HE HAS FOUND US FIRST!

HOLD IT, MAC! IF YOU'RE LOOKIN' FOR A MASQUERADE PARTY, YOU'VE COME TO THE WRONG PLACE! BEAT IT!

WELL SAID, GUARD! WHAT A PITY YOU HAVE NO POWER TO BACK UP SUCH IMPRESSIVE WORDS! YOUR PUNY WEAPONS CANNOT STOP ME!

14.

THEY CAN'T, EH? ONE LITTLE BURST OVER YOUR HEAD WILL SURELY CHANGE YOUR MIND!

HEY! WHA—WHAT GIVES? THE GUN WON'T FIRE! THE TRIGGER SEEMS LOCKED IN PLACE!

I CAN'T EVEN LIFT MY GUN! FEELS LIKE IT WEIGHS A TON!

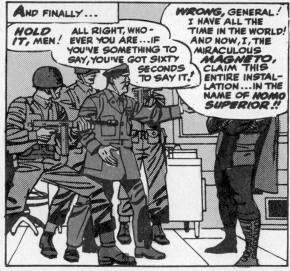

MEANWHILE, IN A DORMITORY ROOM AT THE WORLD'S MOST EXCLUSIVE PRIVATE SCHOOL, JEAN GREY IS ABSORBED WITH HER REFLECTION IN THE FULL-LENGTH MIRROR... THE REFLECTION WHICH REVEALS THE NEW MARVEL GIRL!

MMM, WHOEVER DESIGNED THIS UNIFORM COULD HAVE GIVEN CHRISTIAN DIOR A RUN FOR HIS MONEY!

WHERE DID THE NEW DOLL GO? OH... THERE SHE IS!

WOWEE! LOOKS LIKE SHE WAS POURED INTO THAT UNIFORM!

YOU AGAIN! HONESTLY! CAN'T A GIRL HAVE ANY PRIVACY AROUND HERE?

EASY, GORGEOUS! WE WERE JUST PASSIN' BY! DON'T GO GETTIN' MAD!

SUDDENLY, THE YOUNGSTERS' BANTERING IS FORGOTTEN AS A SHARP COMMANDING THOUGHT REGISTERS IN THE BRAIN OF EACH OF THEM!

ATTENTION, X-MEN! THIS IS PROFESSOR XAVIER! REPORT TO MY STUDY IMMEDIATELY... YOU HAVE FIFTEEN SECONDS! NO EXCUSES WILL BE TOLERATED!

WOW! DID ALL OF YOU RECEIVE THAT MENTAL BLAST?

AND NOW! IT SOUNDED LIKE A TRUMPET'S BLARE! LET'S GO!

EXACTLY FIFTEEN SECONDS LATER...

I COMMEND YOU FOR YOUR PUNCTUALITY!

I HAVE JUST HEARD A BULLETIN ON THE RADIO WHICH CONCERNS YOU!

YOU'RE SPEAKING ALOUD! THAT MEANS IT'S IMPORTANT!

I NEVER SAW THE PROFESSOR LIKE THIS BEFORE ...SO GRIM, SO INTENSE!

A CRISIS HAS OCCURRED AT CAPE CITADEL WHICH LEADS ME TO BELIEVE THE FIRST OF THE EVIL MUTANTS HAS MADE HIS APPEARANCE! THIS WILL BE YOUR BAPTISM OF FIRE! YOU ARE TO GO TO THE CAPE... AND DEFEAT MMM!

YAYBO!! ACTION AT LAST! GANGWAY!

CAPE CITADEL! WHATEVER THE MENACE IS, IT MUST INVOLVE OUR MISSILES!

WONDER WHO THE MUTANT BADDIE IS?

MAN! I CAN GET READY FASTER THAN THE REST OF YOU! ALL I HAVETA DO IS ICE UP AND PUT ON MY BOOTS!

16

AS FOR ME, IT'LL BE A PLEASURE TO GET OUT OF THIS HARNESS I HAVE TO WEAR!

HAVING A PAIR OF WINGS CAN BE MORE TROUBLE THAN YOU'D GUESS!

THESE RESTRAINING BELTS OF MINE KEEP MY WINGS FROM BULGING UNDER MY SUIT, BUT AFTER A WHILE THEY FEEL LIKE I'M WEARING A STRAIT-JACKET!

ANNH! THAT'S MORE LIKE IT! NOW I FEEL LIKE MYSELF AGAIN! NOW THE ANGEL IS READY TO SPREAD HIS WINGS ...AND FLY!

BUT THE TIME HAS NOT YET COME FOR THE ANGEL TO FLY! INSTEAD, THE BAND OF SUPER-HUMAN TEEN-AGERS ARE DRIVEN TO THE AIRPORT IN PROFESSOR XAVIER'S SPECIALLY-BUILT ROLLS ROYCE, WITH ITS DARK-TINTED WINDOWS!

BOY! IT MUSTA TAKEN A HEAP OF GREEN STAMPS TO BY A CHARIOT LIKE THIS!

NO JOKING, PLEASE! CONCENTRATE ON YOUR MISSION! REVIEW YOUR POWERS! YOUR FOE IS CERTAIN TO BE HIGHLY DANGEROUS!

MINUTES LATER, IN THE PROFESSOR'S REMOTE-CONTROL PRIVATE JET, THE X-MEN AND MARVEL GIRL ARE WINGING TOWARDS CAPE CITADEL AT NEARLY THE SPEED OF SOUND!

YOU MEAN THE PROFESSOR IS GUIDING THIS PLANE FROM THE GROUND... BY THOUGHT IMPULSES?! IT'S UN-BELIEVABLE!

LOOK, DOLL... WHEN YOU JOIN THE X-MEN, YOU REALIZE NOTHING'S UN-BELIEVABLE!

A SHORT TIME LATER, AT THE CAPE!...

CEASE FIRING! IT'S USELESS! WE HAVEN'T ANYTHING IN OUR ARSENAL THAT'LL PENETRATE MAGNETO'S MAGNETIC FORCE FIELD!

TO ALL INTENTS AND PURPOSES, HE'S IN FULL CONTROL OF THE INSTALLATION, WHILE WE'RE ON THE OUTSIDE, LOOKING IN!

WITH DUE RESPECT, GENERAL, I REPRESENT THE X-MEN! PERHAPS WE CAN HELP!

X-MEN?! WHAT THE..?!

31

AND NOW, I'LL SWITCH TO *MAXIMUM POWER!* I CAN ONLY MAINTAIN THIS PRESSURE FOR A FEW SECONDS, BUT... *ANH!* I *DID* IT!

BEHIND THE FORCE FIELD, THE NATURAL ENERGY FEED-BACK WEAKENS THE STARTLED *MAGNETO!*

SOME POWER IS ATTACKING ME! SOME POWER AS SUPER-HUMAN AS MY *OWN!*

I WAS STAGGERED BECAUSE I WAS UN-PREPARED FOR ANY SUCH ONSLAUGHT! BUT NOW THAT I'M FOREWARNED, I CAN DEFEAT *ANY* FOE... NO MATTER *HOW* SUPER-HUMAN HE MAY BE!

BUT MAGNETO IS SOON TO LEARN THAT HE HAS MORE THAN ONE FOE TO CONTEND WITH! HE HAS THE FIGHTING BAND OF *X-MEN!*

CYCLOPS ALMOST KNOCKED HIM-SELF OUT, BUT HE GOT US *IN* HERE! NOW LET'S PROVE WE CAN CARRY THE BALL!

LOOK SHARP, *X-MEN!* YOU ARE FACING A DANGER-OUS ENEMY!

AHNN! NOW I SEE MY ANTAGONISTS! FIVE COSTUMED YOUTHS! SURELY ALL THEIR POWERS PUT TOGETHER CAN BE NO MATCH FOR *MINE!*

BUT I WILL LET THE BASE'S *HUNTER MISSILES* DO MY FIGHTING FOR ME! THEY WILL HUNT THE FIVE DOWN, ATTRACTED BY THEIR BODY HEAT!

INTERCEPTOR MISSILES

FIRE

AND SO, AT THE PRESS OF A BUTTON, *MAGNETO* UNLEASHES FIVE OF THE MOST SOPHISTICATED WEAPONS EVER CREATED... ALL ZEROED IN ON THE *X-MEN!*

THE FIRST TARGET FOR THE MERCILESS MISSILES IS THE *ANGEL*, FLYING CLOSEST TO THEM!

GOT TO DODGE THEM, SOMEHOW!

IT'S NO USE! THEY'RE TOO *FAST!* GAINING ON ME....!

HANG ON, ANGEL! I CAN HELP YOU ...WHILE THEY'RE STILL WITHIN RANGE!

THESE *ICE GRENADES* MUSTN'T MISS! THEY'RE THE ANGEL'S ONLY CHANCE!

JUST AS THE HUNTER MISSILES ARE ATTRACTED BY HEAT, SO ARE THE ICEMAN'S ICE GRENADES ATTRACTED BY THE MISSILES' SPEED, AND SO...

BULL'S EYE!

IT *WORKED!* THE ICE COVERED THEIR NOSES, PREVENTING 'EM FROM EXPLODING! NOW, WITH THEIR GUIDANCE SYSTEMS KNOCKED OUT, THEY'VE GOT TO DROP TO THE GROUND!

BUT THERE IS STILL *ONE* MISSILE WHICH WAS NOT HIT...TOO FAR AWAY NOW FOR THE ICEMAN TO ATTACK!

CAN'T KEEP DODGING IT MUCH LONGER!

20.

ANGEL! LOWER... FLY LOWER! COME TOWARDS ME! HURRY!

OKAY, BEAST! BUT WHAT...??

JUST WAIT AND SEE, PAL!

NAH! GOT IT!

GOOD WORK, BEAST! NOW RELEASE IT! I'LL TAKE OVER NOW!

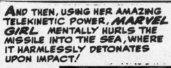

AND THEN, USING HER AMAZING TELEKINETIC POWER, MARVEL GIRL MENTALLY HURLS THE MISSILE INTO THE SEA, WHERE IT HARMLESSLY DETONATES UPON IMPACT!

DESPITE THEIR SEEMING YOUTH AND INEXPERIENCE, THEY ARE MIGHTY ANTAGONISTS! I MUST NEVER AGAIN MAKE THE MISTAKE OF UNDER-ESTIMATING THEM! BUT I SHALL STILL PROVE TO BE THEIR MASTER!

THERE HE IS! I'VE FOUND HIM!! X-MEN, ATTACK!!

WRONG, YOU FLYING FOOL! IT IS I, MAGNETO, WHO HAVE FOUND YOU!

SEE HOW EASILY I CAN STOP YOUR FLIGHT BY MAGNETICALLY HURLING EVERY NEARBY OBJECT WHICH IS NOT BOLTED DOWN!

THE HEAT IS SO INTENSE THAT EVEN *I* CANNOT GET CLOSE TO IT! I MUST WALK CAREFULLY AROUND IT!

THAT *BEAM*... FROM BENEATH THE GROUND!! WHAT...WHAT DOES IT *MEAN*?

IT MEANS YOUR *FINISH*, MAGNETO!

CYCLOPS CREATED A TUNNEL FOR US UNDER THE BLAST WITH HIS ENERGY BEAM... SAVING US FROM THE IMPACT! AND *NOW*...

YOU HAVEN'T DEFEATED ME *YET*! I CAN STILL ESCAPE YOU, FLYING BY MEANS OF MAGNETIC REPULSION!

UGH! HE CREATED ANOTHER MAGNETIC FORCE FIELD! CAN'T FLY THROUGH!

DON'T WORRY, ANGEL! WE'LL BREACH IT IN NO TIME!

AND BREACH IT THEY DO! BUT BY THAT TIME...

HE'S *GONE!* BUT WHERE...?

A MUTANT WITH *HIS* POWERS? HE COULD BE *ANY-WHERE*! BUT AT LEAST WE'VE BEATEN HIM FOR *NOW*!

YOUR BASE IS OPERATIONAL AGAIN, GENERAL! MAGNETO IS GONE!

UNCANNY! YOUR FIFTEEN MINUTES ARE NOT YET UP!

YOU CALL YOURSELVES THE *X-MEN*! I WILL NOT ASK YOU TO REVEAL YOUR TRUE IDENTITIES, BUT I PROMISE YOU THAT BEFORE THIS DAY IS OVER, THE NAME *X-MEN* WILL BE THE MOST HONORED IN MY COMMAND!

THANK YOU, SIR! AND SHOULD AMERICA'S SECURITY EVER AGAIN BE THREAT-ENED, THE *X-MEN* WILL BE BACK!

WELL DONE, STUDENTS! YOU HAVE JUSTIFIED ALL OUR LONG HOURS OF TRAINING...ALL OUR SACRIFICES...ALL OUR DREAMS! AND NOW, RETURN TO ME, MY *X-MEN*!

23.

YOU HAVE JUST FINISHED THE NEWEST, MOST UNUSUAL TALE IN THE ANNALS OF MODERN MAGAZINES! BUT THE BEST IS YET TO COME! FOR FANTASY AT ITS GREATEST, DON'T MISS ISSUE #2 OF *X-MEN*, THE STRANGEST SUPER-HEROES OF ALL!

Three whole decades?

Yep, that's how long it's been since Xavier's titanic team burst upon the comic book world like exploding rockets. And, where once there had been only a handful of mutants, today you need a score-card to keep track of them.

But maybe that's what makes the X-Men the world's most popular superhero team—with all those characters we can never run out of stories.

For the historians among you, our new X-MEN series was launched In 1991. What was different about this particular series? For one thing, it had no adjective in front of the name! For us, that represented a lot of restraint.

Naturally, the adjectiveless X-MEN was a smashing success. And why not? Who could resist a saga of America's most popular mutants battling their arch-enemy, Magneto, who's threatening to destroy the whole human race?

But you've probably recognized that the X-Men offer far more than endless, mindless battle scenes. In fact, I believe the main reason for their ever-growing popularity is the fact that their stories have substance, they're really about something — and that something is centered around the philosophical differences between Xavier and Magneto.

Here's an example. Should mankind strive to live in harmony with those who are "different," or should we consider them enemies and seek to destroy them? Perhaps, in some small way, our X-Men sagas can shine the light of reason upon the gathering darkness of man's intolerance.

Uh-oh, we're getting too heavy. Class dismissed. The excitement's just ahead. . .

STAN LEE PROUDLY PRESENTS
CHRIS CLAREMONT'S *FINAL* ISSUE OF THE X-MEN:

Fallout!

By
CHRIS
CLAREMONT
and JIM
LEE

OFFICIALLY SPEAKING, FIFTY MILES HIGH IS WHERE SPACE BEGINS.

THE BOUNDARY ISN'T THAT PRECISE, OF COURSE; ON A MOLECULAR LEVEL, EARTH'S ATMOSPHERE GOES ON FOR QUITE A WAYS. FOR ALL INTENTS AND PURPOSES THOUGH, THIS IS CONSIDERED TO BE AS HIGH AS HUMAN BEINGS CAN FLY IN ANYTHING LESS THAN A ROCKET.

| SCOTT WILLIAMS | TOM ORZECHOWSKI | JOE ROSAS | BOB HARRAS | TOM DeFALCO |
| INKER | LETTERER | COLORIST | EDITOR | EDITOR IN CHIEF |

A RESTRICTION THAT EVIDENTLY DOES NOT APPLY TO THE *UNCANNY X-MEN.*

I MAY HATE *APOCALYPSE* FOR GRAFTING THESE *BIONIC WINGS* IN PLACE OF THE REAL ONES I WAS BORN WITH...

... BUT I *HAVE* TO ADMIT, STORM, THEY ARE A *PIECE OF WORK.*

WITHOUT THEM, I COULD *NEVER* SOAR SO HIGH, EVEN WITH YOUR *WINDS* TO HELP.

STORM'S REACHED HER LIMIT.

SHE'S FOCUSED HER POWER TO ITS *UTMOST,* BUT THE AIR IS TOO *THIN* AT THIS ALTITUDE TO SUSTAIN EVEN A *GHOST* OF A WIND.

HER BEST IS PLENTY GOOD ENOUGH, RED. SHE'S PULLED THIS GLIDER A FAIR PIECE HIGHER THAN WE EXPECTED.

SHOULD MAKE YOUR JOB THAT MUCH EASIER.

I *HATE* THIS, I *REALLY* HATE THIS.

SHTO?

I MEAN, *FLYING'S* BAD ENOUGH --BUT IN *SPACE?*

AND WHY DOES THE *STUPID* PLANE HAVE TO BE *TRANSPARENT?!*

FORGE SAID IT WAS TO MAKE US FUNCTIONALLY *INVISIBLE,* BOTH TO ELECTRONIC AND OPTICAL SCANNERS.

THAT IS WHY IT IS A *GLIDER...*

I AM AFRAID, MY FRIEND, THIS MAY BE AS FAR AS WE GO.

YEAH, I *KNOW* --WITH NO *METAL* ELEMENTS, SUCH AS *ENGINES,* FOR *MAGNETO* TO DETECT.

YE'D BEST PRAY THE *INDIAN'S* RIGHT, *ICEMAN* ME BOYO, OR WE'RE AS GOOD AS *DEAD.*

WE'VE A PRECIOUS *THIN* CHANCE AS IT IS O' *SAVIN'* THE DAY...

... WHAT WITH OUR *CAPTURED* TEAM-MATES ANNOUNCIN' THEY'VE SWITCHED SIDES AN' *JOINED UP* WITH THE X-MEN'S *ARCH-ENEMY.*

"NOT T' MENTION THE *GREAT POWERS* DOWN BELOW...

"...BOUND-AN'-DETERMINED TO TAKE A MESS AN' TURN IT INTO A ROYAL *CATASTROPHE.*

"NOT SIMPLY FOR US *MUTANTS*, BUT F'R THE WHOLE SAD, SORRY *PLANET!*"

YOU CAN'T DO THIS! SUPPOSE YOU DON'T DESTROY *ASTEROID M*, BUT SIMPLY KNOCK IT OUT OF ORBIT?

ANYONE WANNA IMAGINE THE *DAMAGE* THAT HUNK O' ROCK'LL DO WHEN IT HITS THE GROUND?

THE FIRING TRAJECTORY, *COLONEL FURY*, HAS BEEN CALCULATED TO BLAST THE TARGET *AWAY* FROM EARTH AND INTO DEEP SPACE.

AN' IF THEY'RE WRONG?

YOU WOULD RATHER WE DO *NOTHING*, COLONEL?

I DON'T SEE THE SENSE O' STAMPEDIN' INTO A COURSE OF ACTION WE MAY ALL REGRET.

PLASMA CANNON APPROACHING OPTIMUM FIRING POINT.

YOU'RE A *SOLDIER*, FURY. I'D'VE THOUGHT *YOU*, OF ALL PEOPLE, WOULD UNDERSTAND.

WHAT DO YOU MEAN, CHIEF ANDERSON?

THIS IS A *WAR*, AMBASSADOR KAMANEV!

AND WE EITHER WIN IT OUTRIGHT, OR YIELD OURSELVES-- AND ALL HUMANITY-- UP TO MAGNETO AS VIRTUAL *SLAVES!* ALLOWING HIM TO LORD IT OVER US LIKE SOME ANCIENT GOD ON MOUNT OLYMPUS.

YES, PEOPLE WILL SUFFER AND PEOPLE MAY WELL DIE-- AS MY COUNTRYMEN HERE IN GENOSHA HAVE SUFFERED AND DIED AT THE HANDS OF THAT MUTANT MADMAN AND HIS PET TERRORISTS-- BUT SOMETIMES THAT'S THE PRICE DEMANDED OF SURVIVAL.

AND *FREEDOM!*

MY GOVERNMENT'S POSITION, PRECISELY.

AND YOURS AS WELL, COLONEL FURY.

IN THIS, MOSCOW AND WASHINGTON ARE IN FULL AGREEMENT.

OUR HEADS OF STATE ARE THE *MAKERS* OF POLICY, DR. COOPER.

NO MATTER THE COST?

WE ARE MERELY ITS *EXECUTORS.* AND OUR ORDERS ARE PLAIN.

DIRECTLY THE PLASMA CANNON ACHIEVES ITS FIRING COORDINATES, ASTEROID M-- AND ALL ABOARD--

--ARE TO BE *DESTROYED.*

THEY'RE *SERIOUS.*

THEY'RE *SCARED,* MS. GREY.

IN WAYS WE CAN'T EVEN CONCEIVE OF, BECAUSE-- EVEN THOUGH WE X-MEN ARE THE GOOD GUYS--*WE'RE* THE ONES THEY'RE SCARED OF.

THE FUTURE THEY SEE, JEAN, IS ONE WHERE THEY'RE DESTINED TO BE PERPETUAL *VICTIMS,* INNOCENTS CAUGHT BETWEEN BEINGS WHOSE POWERS THEY BARELY COMPREHEND AND HAVEN'T A HOPE OF MATCHING. WHERE THEY'LL ALWAYS BE AT OUR MERCY.

THIS WAY, THEY DEMONSTRATE THEY MEAN BUSINESS. THEY MAY NEVER BE ABLE TO PUT THE GENETIC GENIE BACK IN ITS BOTTLE, BUT THEY'RE STILL DETERMINED TO BE ITS MASTER.

MUTANTS, SUPER-BEINGS, GODS, ALIENS, A GUY WHO STICKS TO WALLS AT ONE EXTREME, A CREATURE WHO EATS PLANETS AT THE OTHER; EACH ONE THAT COMES INTO BEING, THEY FEEL, DIMINISHES THE REST OF HUMANITY, ORDINARY *HOMO SAPIENS,* THAT LITTLE BIT MORE.

THEY LOOK AROUND, THEY SEE A WORLD THAT'S SLIPPING MORE AND MORE OUT OF THEIR CONTROL.

AND THEREBY PROVE MAGNETO *RIGHT.*

HOW'S YOUR *PSILINK* WITH THE *PROF?* YOU SURE IT CAN'T BE *TAGGED?*

FORGE, I'VE BEEN *CHARLES XAVIER'S* STUDENT SINCE I WAS A CHILD.

WE'RE TELE-PATHICALLY BONDED ON LEVELS NO ONE CAN TOUCH.

THE PROFESSOR IS WELL. BUT THE SITUATION IS AS BAD AS WE FEARED.

...THEY WILL FIGHT US AS TENACIOUSLY AND COU-RAGEOUSLY AS THEY WOULD THEIR DEADLIEST FOES.

CYCLOPS AND HIS TEAM...

... HAVE WHOLEHEARTEDLY EMBRACED MAG-NETO'S CAUSE. AND IF WE DO NOT FOLLOW THEIR LEAD...

BE A MOOT POINT ONCE THAT PLASMA CANNON STARTS TAKING POT-SHOTS.

STORM AND ARCHANGEL ARE THROUGH THE AIRLOCK.

EVERYBODY SEAL YOUR HELMETS AND CHARGE YOUR PRESSURE SUITS.

I'M UP TO IT, FORGE. I HAVE TO BE. THERE'S TOO MUCH AT STAKE.

WHAT COULD THEY BE THINKING OF, USING AN ENERGY WEAPON AGAINST THE MASTER OF MAGNETISM?

ALL THEY'LL DO IS MAKE HIM MAD.

MAD, JEAN, HE MAY ALREADY BE. CERTAINLY CONSUMED BY THE DEMONS THAT HAVE HOUNDED HIM HIS WHOLE LIFE.

GODDESS GRANT US THE OPPORTUNITY TO END HIS MISERY ONCE AND FOR ALL.

COMIN' UP ON SHOWTIME, RED.

AMEN TO THAT, BOSS LADY.

MEANWHILE, EASILY AS FAR ABOVE THE X-MEN'S HEADS...

... AS THEY ARE ABOVE THE SLEEPING, NIGHT-SHROUDED WORLD BELOW...

WHAT ARE YOU DOING, OLD MAN?

SLEEPING?

FORGIVE ME, LORD, TOO EASY AN ANSWER FOR TOO DANGEROUS A MAN.

HE'S YOUR DEADLIEST ENEMY-- WHY NOT USE ON HIM MOIRA MacTAG-GART'S PROCEDURE THAT BOUND HIS PUPILS TO YOUR SIDE?

BECAUSE, MY DEAR CORTEZ, I DO NOT WANT CHARLES XAVIER TURNED.

I WANT HIM **BROKEN!**

NO! WILL Y' NAE LISTEN, EVEN NOW? CHARLES HAD *NOTHING* T'DO WITH WHAT HAPPENED, MAGNETO!

IT WAS *ME*, ACTIN' ON MY OWN, TRYIN' T' FIND A MEANS O' SAVIN' YOUR SOUL--!

I WANT HIS HEART TO CRACK, I WANT HIM TO CHOKE WITH GRIEF--

--AS *I* DID, WHEN I LEARNED OF HOW MY OLD AND DEAR *"FRIEND"* HAD *BETRAYED* ME!

I HAVE TOLD YOU, WOMAN--

--AND WILL NOT DO SO AGAIN--

--YOU WILL SPEAK WHEN SPOKEN TO.

M9MpGK!

AND **NEVER** ON THIS SUBJECT, DO YOU *HEAR?!*

YOU *DARE* CALL YOURSELF A *HUMAN* BEING?!

I WAS A *BABY*, Dr. MacTAGGART, ENTRUSTED *HELPLESS* TO YOUR CHARGE.

YET YOU BETRAYED EVERY CODE OF HONOR AND DECENCY-- EVEN YOUR OWN HIPPOCRATIC OATH AS A PHYSICIAN--

--TO ALTER MY GENETIC STRUCTURE.

DID IT GIVE YOU PLEASURE, PLAYING *GOD?*

HOW YOU MUST HAVE *LAUGHED,* YOU AND XAVIER...

...*PROGRAMMING* ME-- THROUGH, WHAT IS THE PHRASE, *"BEHAVIOR MODIFICATION"*--TO FIT YOUR CONCEPTION OF THE MAN I SHOULD BE.

MAKING EVERY DECISION, EVERY CHOICE I'VE MADE SINCE, A SHAM. MAKING ME LITTLE MORE THAN YOUR *PUPPET!*

ONLY FAIR TURNABOUT, USING THE *SAME* PROCESS ON THE X-MEN. AND FOR THEIR OWN GOOD, TOO *MY* ENDS JUSTIFYING THE MEANS THIS TIME.

THROUGH THEM, I SHALL BRING *PEACE* TO THIS GLOBE.

AND FROM THAT PEACE...

...A GOLDEN AGE--*AKGKH!*

MAGNETO! LET ME *HELP!*

KOFF *KAFF* HARGKGH *KAFF KOFF*

GET *AWAY!*

I *KOFF* WANT *NOTHING KAFF* YOU *KOFF* HAVE TO *KAFF* OFFER.

COME, LORD. LET ME TAKE YOU TO YOUR QUARTERS.

THERE, MY MUTANT POWER WILL RESTORE YOU TO HEALTH AND VIGOR, AS IT HAS BEFORE. AND WILL DO SO FOR AS LONG AS YOU HAVE NEED.

THANK YOU, FABIAN.

I AM IN YOUR DEBT.

NO, MAGNETO, *NO!* DO Y' NOT *SEE?* THE EFFECTS OF EACH *"HEALING"* SESSION WEAR OFF MORE AN' MORE QUICKLY AN' LEAVE YOU MORE AN' MORE DEBILITATED.

AN' HE *KNOWS* IT!

IT'S NOT *KINDNESS FABIAN CORTEZ* IS DOIN' YOU, MAGNETO...

...IT'S DEADLY *HARM!*

46

THINK OF IT AS THE ULTIMATE GRAPPLING HOOK...

...A STRAND OF ENERGY CAST ACROSS THE GULF OF MILES...

...BUT THEN *HOLD FAST* AS JEAN, USING ONLY THE POWER OF HER THOUGHTS AND HER INNATE STRENGTH OF WILL...

...HAULS THE GLIDER UPWARDS, HAND OVER MENTAL HAND...

...KNOWING THAT THE SLIGHTEST SLIP, THE MOST MOMENTARY WEAKNESS, WILL DOOM THEM ALL.

BY HEAVEN--! IF ONLY I COULD ADD MY PSYCHIC STRENGTH TO HERS.

BUT MAGNETO'S *INHIBITORS* PREVENT MY UTILIZING MY OWN PSIONIC POWERS.

"IN THIS CASE, MY DEAR CHILD CAN DEPEND ON NONE BUT HERSELF."

THERE'S SOMETHIN' OUT THERE!

SO FAINT THOUGH I CAN BARELY SEE IT.

...THAT MUST NOT ONLY LATCH ONTO ASTEROID M AS IT SWINGS PAST ALONG ITS ORBITAL TRACK...

COMPANY COMIN', MOIRA?

WOLVERINE! OH NO NO *NO!*

COMIN' TO THE RESCUE, ARE THEY?

CAN'T SAY THAT'S MUCH OF A SURPRISE.

TRANSPARENT PLANE. STORM'S IDEA, FORGE'S DOING, I'LL BET.

VERY SNEAKY. I LIKE THAT.

SNIKT!

BETTER MAKE SURE WE GIVE 'EM THE *WELCOME* THEY DESERVE.

49

YOUR PARDON, SIR, WE ARE HERE TO SEE A MAN ABOUT A RESCUE.

PITY. I WAS HOPING FOR A PIZZA DELIVERY.

IS PROFESSOR XAVIER UNWELL, STORM?

HE IS MAKING A JOKE!

CONTRARY TO POPULAR BELIEF, PETER, THE MAN IS ONLY HUMAN.

COMPLETE WITH A SENSE OF HUMOR.

SUCH AS IT IS.

ET TU, ARCHANGEL?

DON'T I GET RESPECT ANYMORE FROM ANYONE?

LOCATION SECURE, BOSS. SCANNERS CLEAN. INTERNAL ALARMS INERT. SO FAR, SO GOOD.

THAT, I FEAR, PROBABLY WILL NOT LAST.

THE PSYCHIC INHIBITOR FIELD AFFECTS ME THROUGHOUT THE ASTEROID. MY OWN TELEPATHY IS OF NO USE IN FINDING THE OTHERS.

SAME SEEMS TO APPLY TO ME, TOO. I HAVE A SENSE OF YOU, PROFESSOR, NOT THEM.

SO WE FIND 'EM THE OLD-FASHIONED WAY.

NOT NECESSARY, FORGE.

WE'VE ALREADY FOUND YOU!

SO TELL ME, RED--

--IS MY KISS AS MUCH FUN...

...AS WOLVERINE'S?

CYCLOPS!?!

MAKE IT *EASY* ON YOUR-SELVES, *MES BRAVES.*

YOU DON'T WANT THIS ANY MORE THAN *WE,* HEIN?

JOIN US, X-MEN.

AT THE SIDE OF ONE WHO EMBODIES ALL WE *OPPOSE?*

NEVER!

'CAUSE IT MAY WELL BE YOUR *LAST!*

YOUR CHOICE, TIN MAN.

SKRUMP!

THE ACOLYTE DELGADO!

YOUR FUNERAL!

THWAM!

IF I MAY BE SO *BOLD*... ...THAT'S *HARDLY* THE WAY TO INFLUENCE PEOPLE... ...MUCH LESS MAKE *FRIENDS*.

KWUDD!

REVEALING YOUR *TRUE* COLORS, *M'SIEU BETE?*

NO MATTER. WHEN THIS IS FINISHED... ...WE'LL MAKE *SURE* YOU SEE THE LIGHT.

KRAK!

YOUR WAY OR NOTHING, THAT THE TICKET, GAMBIT?

CAST ASIDE THE PAST LIKE A SNAKE SHEDDING ITS SKIN, AS THOUGH IT WAS *NOTHING?*

BLAST THE MAN! HOW CAN HE BE BLOCKING MY *EVERY* SHOT?!

BLAZES, HE'S DEFLECTING THEM BACK AT ME.

SHIELD'S STOPPING MOST--

AKGH!

LAST ONE CLIPPED MY PROSTHETIC LEG. ONLY A SURFACE STRIKE, THOUGH, NO MAJOR DAMAGE.

CAJUN'S *NAILED*, FORGE.

STORM'S GOING AFTER ROGUE, ANYONE ELSE DOWN HERE NEED A HAND?

BOOP!

ONLY *ONE* PERSON AT THE MOMENT, ICEMAN.

REGRETTABLY, THOUGH, ANY POSSIBLE DELIVERANCE FROM YOUR TEAM-MATES...

YOU!

...WILL COME TOO LATE!

Wugh!

BUT PSYLOCKE'S OUT-SMARTED HERSELF. FOR WHILE HER *PSYCHIC KNIFE* DOES INDEED DISRUPT THE STRUCTURE OF ICEMAN'S BRAIN...

...IT ALSO TRIGGERS AN UN-CONTROLLABLE, BROAD-BAND OUTBURST OF ENERGY FROM HIM THAT LEAVES EVERYTHING IN CLOSE PROXIMITY SHEETED IN ICE -- INCLUDING *HER.*

MEANWHILE...

TK'S STILL TOO WEAK TO DEFEND MYSELF.

MY *TELEPATHY'S* ALLOWING ME TO ANTICIPATE SCOTT'S TARGETS A SPLIT-SECOND BEFORE HE FIRES...

...BUT I CAN'T MAINTAIN THIS PACE. MY BODY'S TIRING TOO MUCH TO KEEP DODGING HIS *OPTIC BLASTS.*

CYCLOPS-- ALL OF YOU--

--STOP!

ROGUE, WHAT ARE YOU *DOING?!*

HAVE YOU *BETRAYED* THE CAUSE, TOO?!!

ZARK!

WAIT--

--THIS IS INSANE--

--WHAT AM I DOING?!

AIN'T ALT'GETHER SURE MYSELF...

...'CEPT WE'RE SIDIN' WITH OUR DEADLIEST FOES AGAINST OUR NEAREST AN' DEAREST...

...AN' THAT AIN'T NATURAL!

THAT, ROGUE, AS WITH SO MANY THINGS...

...DEPENDS ON YOUR POINT-OF-VIEW.

I SHOULD HAVE KNOWN *NO* POWER COULD *BIND* YOU X-MEN-- YOUR INNATE STRENGTH OF CHARACTER IS TOO STRONG-- EVEN WHEN IT IS FOR YOUR OWN *GOOD*...

...BUT I HAD *HOPED.*

"GOOD"?! MISTER, YOU DON'T KNOW THE *MEANING* OF THE WORD!

WHAT I DID, CYCLOPS, I DID TO *SAVE* YOU!

BY MAKING US YOUR *PUPPETS*?!

YOU WERE *WARNED,* X-MAN!

EITHER STAND *WITH* THE *MASTER*--

--OR *FALL* BEFORE HIM!

NO, DON'T!

POW POW POW

55

GAME'S OVER, BUB.

TIME T' CALL IT QUITS.

GO AHEAD THEN, WOLVERINE.

MAKE YOUR DAY. PLAY THE ROLE YOU SEEM BORN TO...

...THAT OF EXECUTIONER.

I... CANNOT STOP YOU.

I'M TEMPTED.

BUT WE'RE HEROES. EVEN WHEN IT HURTS, WE GOTTA STAND FOR SOMETHING.

AN' I DRAW THE LINE AT MURDER.

MY PROCESS WAS A FAILURE, MAGNETO-- EFFECTIVE ONLY SO LONG AS THE SUBJECT NEVER USED THEIR MUTANT POWER.

THE STRUCTURES OF MIND AND BODY HAVE T' BE ALIGNED A CERTAIN, SPECIFIC WAY FOR THOSE POWERS T' OPERATE, IN HARMONY SO T' SPEAK WI' YUIR ESSENTIAL CHARACTER.

THAT'S WHY YOU ALL HAVE SUCH INDOMITABLE WILLS.

NO MATTER HOW DEEPLY YE'RE "BRAINWASHED," EACH USE O' YUIR POWER REVERTS YOU TO YUIR NATURAL, "DEFAULT" STATE.

YOU WERE NEVER DEPRIVED OF ANYTHING BY ME. THE CHOICES YOU MADE WERE THE ONES Y' WOULD HAVE MADE, REGARDLESS.

AN' IF THERE'S BEEN BETRAYAL HERE, 'TIS NAE BY US. LOOK T' YUIR OWN F'R THAT.

LOOK T' THE MAN WHO'S GOADED YOU T' CONFRONTATION AT EVERY STAGE, WHO'S CAST YOU IRREVOCABLY AS HUMANITY'S ENEMY!

CLAIMIN' HIS POWER WAS HEALIN' YOU, WHEN EVERY USE OF IT MADE MATTERS WORSE!

WHAT CORTEZ DID WAS AMPLIFY YUIR OWN POWER TO EFFECT THE ILLUSION O' RECOVERY. Y' WERE NO LESS HURT THAN BEFORE, Y' SIMPLY DID NA NOTICE IT ANY LONGER.

EVENTUALLY, P'RHAPS EVEN NOW, Y'D REACH A POINT O' NO RETURN, BEYOND YUIR POWER'S ABILITY T' SUSTAIN THE PHYSICALITY THA' HOUSES IT.

Y' NEEDN'T WORRY ABOUT WOLVERINE, MAN, I FEAR Y'RE DYIN' ALREADY.

N' YOU LIE!

COULD BE, BUB.

BUT THEN--WHO'S THAT BUGGIN' OUT IN THE ESCAPE POD?

WE TRIED TO STOP HIM--THAT'S WHY I WAS SO LATE GETTIN' HERE-- BUT YOUR ASTEROID'S TOO FLAMIN' BIG. GOT TO THE HATCH TOO LATE.

HE IS FLEEING BEFORE THE PLASMA CANNON IS FIRED!

WHAT PLASMA CANNON?

THE CANNON, CHUMPS, THAT'S GOING TO *BLAST* YOU OUT OF SPACE.

AND, SADLY, LORD MAGNETO, YOU TOO MUST PAY THE PRICE.

BUT YOU WILL LIVE ON IN THE MINDS OF MEN LIKE ME--

--TO INFLAME AND INSPIRE US--

--TO FOLLOW OUR RIGHTEOUS CAUSE--

--THAT *OUR* PEOPLE MAY NOT FADE FROM THE *EARTH!*

THUS-- I MUST PUSH THE PROCESS ALONG!

MISSION CONTROL-- EMERGENCY-- SOME OUTSIDE INFLUENCE HAS TAKEN OVER OUR CONTROL CIRCUITS!

THE CANNON IS *FIRING!*

WITH, AS PREDICTED, AS FEARED, DEVASTATING RESULTS.

THE BEAM BURNS THROUGH SOLID ROCK AS THOUGH THE ASTEROID HAD NO MORE SUBSTANCE THAN A CLOUD.

AND BECAUSE ITS INTERNAL SYSTEMS-- INDEED, IN SOME MEASURE, THE PHYSICAL FABRIC OF THE PLANETOID-- ARE LINKED WITH MAGNETO HIMSELF...

...HE IS STRUCK AS HARD, PERHAPS EVEN AS FATALLY, AS HIS HOME.

A... MASTERFUL STRATAGEM. IN ADDITION TO THE PLASMA BEAM, CORTEZ ATTEMPTED TO SIMULTANEOUSLY IGNITE THE NUCLEAR WARHEADS...

...OF THE MISSILES I HAD ARRAYED ABOUT MY ASTEROID AS A DEFENSIVE MEASURE.

I HAVE MAGNETICALLY... DISABLED THE TRIGGERS. THE WEAPONS ARE USELESS.

TIME T' GO, FOLKS.

FAST AS WE CAN!

I'LL HELP JEAN!

ROGUE, TAKE THE PROFESSOR!

YOU ARE THE STUBBORNEST OF MEN, CHARLES...

...NOT TO MENTION ONE OF THE MOST FOOLISH!

AND MAGNETO AS WELL, CYCLOPS!

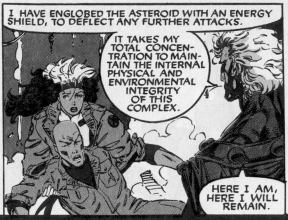

I HAVE ENGLOBED THE ASTEROID WITH AN ENERGY SHIELD, TO DEFLECT ANY FURTHER ATTACKS.

IT TAKES MY TOTAL CONCENTRATION TO MAINTAIN THE INTERNAL PHYSICAL AND ENVIRONMENTAL INTEGRITY OF THIS COMPLEX.

HERE I AM, HERE I WILL REMAIN.

IF YOU WON'T SAVE YOURSELF, AT LEAST THINK OF YOUR FOLLOWERS.

THERE'S ROOM IN THE X-WING, COME WITH US, I BEG YOU!

NO.

THEY HAVE MADE THEIR FREE CHOICE, CHARLES. SO HAVE I.

MY LIFE WAS SHAPED BY FORCES AND EVENTS NONE OF YOU CAN POSSIBLY UNDERSTAND.

YOU SPEAK TO THE BEST IN HUMANITY. I HAVE ENDURED THE WORST.

YOU IMAGINE THE REALITY OF THE HOLOCAUST, OF THE NAZI DEATH CAMPS. I GREW UP IN ONE.

PERHAPS, AS YOU SAY, I AM TAINTED BY BLOOD AND RAGE-- AND DEATH.

BUT PERHAPS AS WELL, THAT BLOOD AND RAGE AND DEATH COMPRISE THE ARMOR THAT WILL SUSTAIN ME AND THOSE WHO STAND BY ME THROUGH THE ORDEAL TO COME.

THE PAST IS PROLOGUE, OLD FRIEND. AND THE FUTURE I BEHOLD FOR YOU IS...

...WAR.

WE HAVE ALREADY CHOSEN OUR PATH.

CHOSEN WHAT-- A LEGACY TO OUR CHILDREN OF UNENDING CONFLICT?

ARE YOUR HEART AND SOUL SO BLACK?

PROFESSOR, WE GOTTA GO!

IT'S NO USE TALKIN', AH SEE THAT NOW.

Y'ALL MAY USE THE SAME WORDS, BUT YOU DON'T SPEAK THE SAME LANGUAGE. AH WONDER IF Y'EVER DID.

LEAVE ME BE, ROGUE! I WON'T PERMIT THIS!

THAT DECISION, CHARLES, IS NOT YOURS TO MAKE.

FAREWELL, MY OLD FRIEND.

WHATEVER COMES, I AND MINE WILL NOT GO LIKE LAMBS TO THE SLAUGHTER-- BUT LIKE TIGERS.

WE'RE ABOARD, STORM! HATCH IS SEALED TIGHT!

GET US OUTTA HERE!

NO-- MAGNETO-- THIS ISN'T THE ANSWER, IT ISN'T THE WAY--

"NO!

AT THE LAST...

...HE OPENED HIS THOUGHTS TO ME.

HE IS STILL THE MAN I REMEMBER FROM YOUNGER, *HAPPIER* DAYS-- WHO WAS MY *FRIEND*-- AND YET...

...NONE OF THAT MATTERS ANYMORE, DOES IT?

"I SAVE YOU, X-MEN," HE SAID, "BECAUSE THAT IS MY TASK IN LIFE:

"...TO SAFEGUARD MY PEOPLE-- HOMO SAPIENS SUPERIOR-- MUTANTKIND--FROM THOSE WHO WOULD DO US HARM.

"AND THOSE FORCES ARE LEGION.

"IN THAT, AND I SUSPECT NOTHING ELSE, CHARLES, WE ARE MUCH ALIKE.

"I HAVE SURVIVED *ONE* HOLOCAUST, I COULD NOT TOLERATE ANOTHER. NOR ANY WHO-- BY ACCIDENT, BY INTENT-- ACT TO BRING IT ABOUT.

"I BORE NO ANIMUS TO YOU, OLD FRIEND, OR YOUR STUDENTS, UNTIL YOU CHOSE TO OPPOSE ME.

"THEN, I HAD NO CHOICE BUT TO COUNT YOU AMONG MY ENEMIES. HAVE NO ILLUSIONS ON THAT SCORE.

"...FOR IF WE WERE EVER TO MEET AGAIN...

"PERHAPS IT'S BEST IT END THIS WAY, CHARLES. BEST FOR MY DREAM TO END IN FLAMES AND GLORY, HERE FAR ABOVE EARTH...

"...I WOULD HAVE SHOWN YOU NO MERCY.

"I GIVE YOU YOUR DREAM, CHARLES. BUT I FEAR, IN TIME, YOUR HEART WILL *BREAK*, AS YOU REALIZE IT HAS EVER BEEN A FOOL'S HOPE. FAREWELL, MY FRIEND."

GOTTA SAY THIS FOR THE MAN--

--HE KNOWS HOW TO MAKE AN *EXIT*.

YOU DID WRONG, MOIRA. WE ARE NOT GODS, THOUGH OUR POWERS MAKE SOME THINK DIFFERENTLY. WE HAVE NO RIGHT TO TAMPER WITH ANOTHER'S INNER BEING.

BUT YOU ARE ALSO NOT TO BLAME.

AS MAGNETO HIMSELF SAID, THE FORCES THAT SHAPED HIM...

...DID THEIR WORK LONG BEFORE THE X-MEN WERE EVEN BORN.

NOW PERHAPS THE TIME HAS COME TO DO SOME SHAPING OF OUR OWN.

TO *ACT* ON THE STAGE OF HISTORY.

LIKE MAGETO, WE HAVE MADE CHOICES IN OUR LIVES, WE HAVE TAKEN OUR STAND FOR WHAT *WE* BELIEVE IN. WE WERE BOTH HAUNTED MEN, HIM BY A *NIGHTMARE*, ME BY A *DREAM*.

TIME WILL TELL WHICH OF US WAS *RIGHT*.

HIS CHOICE WAS EVER FUELED BY RAGE, TAINTED BY THE *DESPAIR* THAT SCARS HIS SOUL.

AS OURS, I PRAY, WILL BE SUSTAINED BY *HOPE*.

WE HAVE IT WITHIN OURSELVES, X-MEN-- AS DO ALL PEOPLE, WHETHER MUTANTS OR NO-- TO LEAVE OUR WORLD BETTER THAN WE FOUND IT.

TO STRIVE FOR THE HEIGHTS OF OUR POTENTIAL, TO SEEK OUT THE *BEST* IN OURSELVES AND IN OTHERS, WHERE MAGNETO WOULD HAVE AUTOMATICALLY ASSUMED THE *WORST*.

YES, THAT IS AN IDEAL. PERHAPS AN UNATTAINABLE ONE. BUT SUCCESS IN THIS IS NOT WHAT IS IMPORTANT.

WHAT MATTERS IS THE ATTEMPT. AND OUR POWERS, OUR ROLE AS *HEROES*-- PERHAPS EVEN THE SIMPLE FACT THAT WE *LIVE*-- GIVES US THE OBLIGATION TO *TRY*.

CSC · 1976-1991 · FIN

NEXT: OMEGA RED!

61

PART TWO

WHEN THE GOLDEN AVENGER WAS GRAY

MARVEL Comics has never been very much into politics. Today, with more than a dozen different writers scripting the largest line of comicbooks in the world, we still have no official party line—I issue no editorial edicts as to what the political tone of our stories should be. Actually, most of our writers are young, idealistic, and passionately liberal. Some are a bit more reserved, a bit more middle-of-the-road. The same goes for our artists, who also contribute a great deal to the basic plotting and structure of our tales. They include every shade and facet of the political spectrum, and that's the way it should be. After all, the Marvel Bullpen is really America in microcosm, and I figure that, like our nation itself, we should be strong enough and wise enough to tolerate every type of ideology. The only philosophies that have no place at Marvel are those preaching war or bigotry.

In case you're wondering what all this profoundly serious jazz has to do with the origins of Marvel's superheroes, let me humbly hasten to explain. The next pictorial production that you're about to passionately peruse is set against the background of the war in Vietnam. For purposes of the story, there's a North Vietnamese general who's the very epitome of a comicbook bad guy. The good guy is a noble American helping the noble Vietnamese battle the sinister Commies from the north.

Now it's important that you bear in mind that this yarn was written in 1963, at a time when most of us genuinely felt that the conflict in that tortured land really was a simple matter of good versus evil and that the American military action against the Viet Cong was tantamount to St. George's battle against the dragon. Since that time, of course, we've all grown up a bit, we've realized that life isn't quite so simple, and we've been trying to extricate ourselves from the tragic entanglement of Indochina.

There's another aspect to the tale that follows that might be worthy of mention. In our eternal effort to create original and innovative superheroes, I had been toying with one idea that had haunted me for months. As far as I knew, there had never been a major costumed comicbook character who was a wealthy and successful businessman. Such a background would have been considered too trite and too pedestrian for a hero who dealt in feats of derring-do. And yet, the more I thought about it the more it grabbed me. I could envision a Howard Hughes type with almost unlimited wealth— a man with holdings and interests in every part of the world—envied by other males and sought after by glamorous females from every walk of life. But, like virtually all the mixed-up Marvel heroes, he'd have to be flawed. There'd have to be some tragic element to his life to provide the necessary dimension of realism—some Achilles heel to make the reader feel pity even while envying him.

The more I thought about it the more the concept fascinated me. We would create a character who seemed to have everything a man could wish for—wealth, fame, good looks, success. He'd be a playboy, a tycoon, a man's man. But he'd have some secret sorrow, some secret life-and-death problem that would plague and torment him each day of his life. And the more I thought about it, the faster it all came together.

What if our hero had an injured heart—a heart that required him to wear some sort of metal device to keep it beating? The metal device could be the basic element in an entire suit of armor which could both power him and conceal his identity. I loved it. It had the right ring to it. I knew it would work.

Now it was time to discuss the project with whichever artist would do the illustrations. A writer can only go so far in conceptualizing, and then he needs his creation to take form within the story's panels. Luckily, we had the perfect artist available at that time—Dazzlin' Donnie Heck, whose style had both a crispness and a sophistication that would be perfect for the strip I had in mind. Don had been with us for years, doing virtually every type of feature imaginable: mystery tales, romance stories, fantasy yarns, monster epics; you name it, he's done it. All I had to do was describe the project and Don was all for it. Now what we needed was a name.

Needless to say, the title of a strip is tremendously important. It must be a name that has an appealing lilt to it, implies action and adventure, and sounds dramatic. Sometimes it can take longer to dream up a title than it takes to write and draw the entire story. I'm sure you can appreciate the problem. What were we to call our newest character? *The Adventures of Rich Man*? Hardly. *Super-Financier*? Not quite. *The Mighty Industrialist*? It seemed to lack something. *The Mysterious Metal Heart*? Yechh! But wait a minute. If he's going to wear a type of metal armor, that could be it. The word "metal" was a step in the right direction. How about *Metal Man*? Not bad, but somehow it didn't seem strong enough. Some metals are weak—some can bend and break. I felt it would be better to get a specific metal. Perhaps steel would do the trick. But it didn't quite work in combination with other words, as in *Steel Man*—the rhythm was wrong. So, I kept thinking and running down a list of metals until I came to—iron! The minute I said it, I knew we had our name. *Iron Man!* The sound was perfect. It suggested might, and raw power. It was easy to say and it sounded dramatic. I couldn't wait to rush to the typewriter.

But alas, I had to wait. Just as I was about to start the first script, a minor deadline emergency came up and I had to write a new *Spider-Man* instead. But I didn't want to wait, didn't want to waste another hour before starting work on *Iron Man,* in case one of the other comicbook companies beat us to the title. Any time we dream up anything new, we live in constant fear that one of our competitors will hear about it and rush out a hastily-produced version with the same name to grab the copyright. Most comicbook people are slightly paranoid in this respect—and some of us with good reason. At any rate, it was easy for me to solve the problem. Laughin' Larry Lieber happened to be in the Bullpen at the time, and he also happened to be between scripts just then. Eagerly I pounced on him, told him the plot, headed him toward the nearest typewriter, chained him to a chair, and the rest is history.

But, before unleashing you upon the phantasmagoric pleasures that lie ahead, I must prepare you for some unexpected revelations. (See how subtly I seek to hold your interest by implying that there are surprises to come. I hate myself for employing so devious a device, but 'tis merely the recidivist result of lo these many years of writing comics.) As your grateful eyes behold the beauty of the strip that follows, dazzled though you may be by the text, and the art, and the imaginative imagery that await you, still you are certain to notice that the Iron Man you are now encountering is not the same Iron Man whom you have come to know and love. His armor is far more bulky, and its color is a dull gray rather than the glistening and glittering gold of today. Indeed, like so many sensational strips in the mighty Marvel galaxy of stars, Iron Man has been continually changing, evolving, improving until it has become the peerless production that enthralls you each month.

However, since this proud volume is the second in a series that shall constitute a living history of Marvel Comics, it behooves us to present the origin of Iron Man exactly as it appeared on that fateful day in the year 1963. Historians of the future must know that they can trust this book, have faith in its pictures, and treat its text as gospel. That is why today's graceful Golden Avenger is herewith depicted as a lumbering, gray-garbed behemoth, exactly as the cheering hordes of Marveldom beheld him when he made his first appearance.

And now, return with us to an earlier day—to the time when Tony Stark and his tiny transistors took the comicbook world by storm.

IN A SECLUDED AREA SOMEWHERE IN THE U.S. DEFENSE PERIMETER, THERE STANDS A CLOSELY GUARDED BUILDING... THE LABORATORY OF ANTHONY STARK!

BOY! THAT GUY STARK MUST REALLY **RATE**, TO GET A TWENTY-FOUR HOUR GUARD!

HE **RATES**, ALL RIGHT! THE COMMIES WOULD GIVE THEIR **EYETEETH** TO KNOW WHAT HE'S WORKING ON NOW!

AND, INSIDE...

GENERAL, YOU WILL SEE MY TINY TRANSISTOR INCREASE THE POWER OF THIS SMALL MAGNET SO TREMENDOUSLY, THAT IT WILL OPEN THAT LOCKED VAULT!

OH, COME NOW, STARK! THAT JUST ISN'T **POSSIBLE**!

THINK SO? THERE! I'VE SWITCHED ON THE TRANSISTOR! IT'S ENERGIZING THE MAGNET!

CLICK

THE DOOR --IT'S BEGINNING TO BUDGE!

NATURALLY! MY TINY TRANSISTORS ARE **SO** POWERFUL THAT...

-- THEY CAN INCREASE THE FORCE OF **ANY** DEVICE...

--A THOUSANDFOLD!

CRACK

NOW DO YOU BELIEVE THAT THE TRANSISTORS I'VE INVENTED ARE CAPABLE OF SOLVING YOUR PROBLEM IN VIETNAM?

STARK, AFTER WHAT I'VE JUST SEEN, I'M READY TO BELIEVE **ANYTHING**!

YES, IT **WAS** AN AMAZING DEMONSTRATION! BUT NOW, LET US LEARN **MORE** ABOUT THE MAN WHOSE GENIUS MADE IT POSSIBLE! LET US LEARN MORE ABOUT ANTHONY STARK, THE ONE WHO IS FATED TO BECOME... **IRON MAN**!

69

ANTHONY STARK... RICH, HANDSOME, KNOWN AS A GLAMOROUS PLAYBOY, CONSTANTLY IN THE COMPANY OF BEAUTIFUL, ADORING WOMEN...

LOOK! THERE'S TONY STARK!

UMMMNN... HE'S THE DREAMIEST THING THIS SIDE OF ROCK HUDSON!

THE RIVIERA WAS A REAL DRAG TILL **YOU** SHOWED UP, DARLING!

YES, ANTHONY STARK IS BOTH A SOPHISTICATE AND A SCIENTIST! A MILLIONAIRE BACHELOR, AS MUCH AT HOME IN A LABORATORY AS IN HIGH SOCIETY!

BUT, THIS MAN WHO SEEMS SO FORTUNATE, WHO'S ENVIED BY MILLIONS -- IS SOON DESTINED TO BECOME THE MOST TRAGIC FIGURE ON EARTH!

OUR TALE REALLY HAS ITS BEGINNING HALFWAY AROUND THE WORLD, IN A SOUTH VIETNAM JUNGLE, MENACED BY **WONG-CHU**, THE RED GUERRILLA TYRANT!

HAH! I HAVE BROUGHT **ANOTHER** VILLAGE TO ITS KNEES!

NOW FOR THE WRESTLING MATCH! IF ANY PRISONER CAN DEFEAT WONG-CHU, I FREE WHOLE VILLAGE!

DESPERATE TO SAVE THEIR VILLAGE, THE STRONGEST OF THE NATIVES ACCEPTS THE WAR LORD'S CHALLENGE...

AH, YOU ARE GOOD! BUT WONG-CHU **BETTER!**

ANOTHER, AND ANOTHER, TRIES IN VAIN...

I AM STRONGEST OF ALL! NEXT TO **WONG-CHU** OTHER MEN ARE BUT **FLEAS!**

IT IS OVER! NOW LET US PLUNDER THE TOWN! FOR **NONE** CAN STOP THE VICTORIOUS WONG-CHU!

3

IN A FEW DAYS SHRAPNEL WILL REACH HIS HEART-- THEN HE WILL DIE! NOTHING CAN SAVE HIM!

BAH! WE CAN USE HIS GENIUS! WONG-CHU WILL TRICK HIM INTO SPENDING HIS LAST DAYS ON EARTH WORKING FOR US! IS HE STRONG ENOUGH NOW?

YES, HE CAN WORK TILL SHRAPNEL REACHES HEART!

WE KNOW YOU ARE AMERICAN WEAPONS INVENTOR! IF YOU DESIGN POWERFUL NEW WEAPON FOR ME, AFTER-WARDS I HAVE SURGEON SAVE YOUR LIFE!

HE'S LYING... IF THEY COULD THEY'D DO IT NOW, TO BE SURE I LIVE LONG ENOUGH TO DESIGN WEAPONS FOR THEM!

I KNOW I'VE ONLY DAYS TO LIVE, BUT MY LAST ACT WILL BE TO DEFEAT THIS GRINNING, SMIRKING, RED TERRORIST!

ALL RIGHT, WONG-CHU, I'LL DO IT!

I KNEW YOU WOULD NOT HESITATE TO BETRAY YOUR COUNTRY TO SAVE YOURSELF!

HERE ROOM WHERE YOU WORK! PLENTY OF SCRAP IRON! PLENTY TOOLS!

THIS I PROMISE YOU... I SHALL BUILD THE MOST FANTASTIC WEAPON OF ALL TIME!

I'LL BUILD IT, ALL RIGHT, BUT IT WILL BE MINE...

--MADE FOR ONLY ONE PURPOSE-- TO KEEP ME ALIVE!

CLICK!

EVERY TICK OF THE CLOCK BRINGS THE DEADLY PIECE OF SHRAPNEL CLOSER TO MY HEART! I'VE GOT TO WORK FASTER THAN I'VE EVER WORKED BEFORE! CAN'T AFFORD A SINGLE MISTAKE!

THEN, ON THE SECOND DAY OF TONY STARK'S RACE AGAINST TIME...

THIS OLD ONE, PROFESSOR YINSEN! ONCE GREAT SCIENTIST! NOW LOWLY MAN-SERVANT OF WONG-CHU... ...WILL HELP YOU BUILD WEAPON!

NO! I WILL NEVER HELP THE EVIL RED TYRANTS! NEVER!!

PROFESSOR YINSEN, IN COLLEGE I READ YOUR BOOKS! YOU WERE THE GREATEST PHYSICIST OF ALL!! THEN, EVERYONE THOUGHT YOU HAD DIED!

I'D HAVE BEEN BETTER OFF IF I HAD! I WAS PRESSED INTO SLAVE LABOR BY THE REDS, AND WHEN I RESISTED, WONG-CHU TOOK ME PRISONER!

NO LONGER ABLE TO WORK IN SECRET, ANTHONY STARK MUST REVEAL HIS PLAN TO THE AGED SCHOLAR, THE ONLY HUMAN HE DARES TRUST!

AN IRON MAN! FANTASTIC! A MIGHTY, ELECTRONIC BODY, TO KEEP YOUR HEART BEATING AFTER THE SHRAPNEL REACHES IT! WE JUST MIGHT SUCCEED! THINK WHAT A CREATURE WE COULD CREATE! WHAT WONDERS HE SHALL PERFORM!

AND THE REDS THEMSELVES GAVE US ALL THE MATERIALS WE WILL NEED!

THUS, A DYING MAN'S DESPERATE RACE AGAINST TIME CONTINUES...

I'VE DONE EXTENSIVE WORK WITH TRANSISTORS! I CAN DESIGN THEM IN ANY SIZE TO PERFORM ANY FUNCTION!

WE SHALL USE THEM TO OPERATE THE MACHINE ELECTRONICALLY TO MOVE COUNTLESS GEARS AND CONTROL LEVERS!

ALL ACTIVITY MUST BE COORDINATED PERFECTLY! THE IRON FRAME MUST DUPLICATE EVERY ACTION OF THE HUMAN BODY!

IT SHALL, MY FRIEND! IT SHALL! THIS SHALL BE THE CROWNING ACHIEVEMENT OF MY LIFE!

HOURS PASS INTO DAYS, AS THE SHRAPNEL MOVES CLOSER AND CLOSER TO ANTHONY STARK'S HEART...

I CAN FEEL THE PRESSURE! MY TIME IS RUNNING OUT! WE MUST WORK FASTER!

THERE! THE SELF-LUBRICATION SYSTEM IS COMPLETED! JUST A LITTLE LONGER! YOU MUST HAVE COURAGE!

AND THEN, WHEN THE DOOMED AMERICAN'S CONDITION BECOMES CRITICAL -- WHEN HE CAN NO LONGER STAND...

THE LIFE-GIVING HEART OF YOUR IRON BODY IS READY! QUICKLY,... CLAMP IT AROUND YOUR CHEST!

THERE! IT IS DONE! WHEN I ACTIVATE THE MACHINE, YOUR OWN AMAZING TRANSISTORS WILL FURNISH THE POWER TO KEEP YOUR HEART BEATING! YOU SHOULD LIVE AS LONG AS THE IRON BODY OPERATES!

THIS GENERATOR WILL SOON BUILD UP ENOUGH ENERGY TO FURNISH ALL THE POWER YOU'LL NEED TO MOVE!

BUT SUDDENLY...

THE WARNING LIGHT WE INSTALLED-- IT FLASHES! SOMEONE IS APPROACHING!

IT MUST BE WONG-CHU! IF HE ENTERS NOW, ALL OUR WORK WILL HAVE BEEN IN VAIN!!

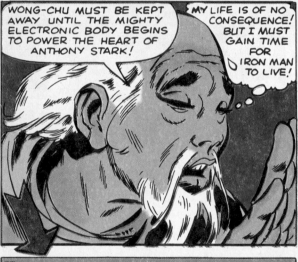

WONG-CHU MUST BE KEPT AWAY UNTIL THE MIGHTY ELECTRONIC BODY BEGINS TO POWER THE HEART OF ANTHONY STARK!

MY LIFE IS OF NO CONSEQUENCE! BUT I MUST GAIN TIME FOR IRON MAN TO LIVE!

THEN, BEFORE THE REDS CAN ENTER THE ROOM, THE BRAVE PROFESSOR YINSEN MAKES ONE DESPERATE LAST EFFORT...

DEATH TO WONG-CHU! DEATH TO THE EVIL TYRANT!

HE HAS GONE MAD! AFTER HIM! END HIS MISERABLE LIFE! HE IS OF NO FURTHER USE TO ME!

SLAM!

CLICK!

AND THUS THE GALLANT CHINESE SCIENTIST BUYS PRECIOUS SECONDS FOR ANTHONY STARK, WHILE THE LIFE-SUSTAINING MACHINE BUILDS UP MORE AND MORE POWER BEHIND THE LOCKED DOOR!!!

BANG!

IT IS DONE! DRAG HIM AWAY!

YOU WILL NOT HAVE DIED IN VAIN, MY FRIEND! I SWEAR IT! THE IRON MAN SWEARS IT!

THEN, EVEN AS PROFESSOR YINSEN BREATHES HIS LAST, THE ELECTRONIC MARVEL BEGINS TO STIR...

THE TRANSISTORS HAVE SUFFICIENT ENERGY NOW! MY HEART IS BEATING NORMALLY! THE MACHINE IS KEEPING ME ALIVE! **ALIVE!!**

AND THE TRANSISTOR-POWERED CIRCUITS ARE COORDINATED WITH MY BRAIN WAVES, JUST AS ANY LIVING HUMAN'S BRAIN CONTROLS HIS OWN BODY!

B-BUT I'M LOSING MY BALANCE!

THUD!

I'M LIKE A BABY LEARNING TO WALK! BUT I HAVEN'T **TIME!** I MUST LEARN QUICKLY! I MUST GET THE KNACK OF MANIPULATING THIS MASSIVE, UNBELIEVABLY POWERFUL IRON SHELL BEFORE THE REDS FIND ME -- OR ELSE I'LL BE AT THEIR MERCY!

BUT THE BRAIN WHICH HAS MASTERED THE SECRETS OF SCIENCE IS ALSO CAPABLE OF MASTERING ITS NEW BODY! AND SO...

I HAVE THE FEEL OF IT NOW.! I CAN STAND-- MOVE-- EVEN **WALK** WITHOUT TOPPLING!

MEANWHILE, OUTSIDE THE LOCKED DOOR...

BREAK IT DOWN! **SMASH IT!** I MUST LEARN WHAT HAS HAPPENED IN THERE!

WHAM WH

8

THEY'RE COMING! THIS IS MY GREATEST TEST! CAN THE THING I HAVE CREATED SURVIVE? THE THING WHICH IS LESS THAN HUMAN...YET, FAR MORE THAN MERELY HUMAN! THIS THING WHICH IS NOW-- ANTHONY STARK!!

WHAM

MY BRAIN STILL THINKS! MY HEART STILL BEATS! BUT, IN ORDER TO REMAIN ALIVE, I MUST SPEND THE REST OF MY LIFE IN THIS IRON PRISON!!

BUT, THIS BITTER REALIZATION IS SUDDENLY INTERRUPTED, AS THE IRON MAN SNAPS BACK TO REALITY...

THEY'LL SOON BE THRU THE DOOR... I MUST CONCEAL MYSELF UNTIL I CAN PLAN MY NEXT MOVE!

FORTUNATELY, YINSEN AND I EQUIPPED MY IRON BODY WITH MANY ATTACHMENTS, SUCH AS THESE!

I'LL FASTEN THESE SUCTION CUPS TO MY PALMS AND TURN ON MY TRANSISTOR-POWERED AIR-PRESSURE JETS!

THEY WORK! THEY GIVE ME THE POWER TO SOAR INTO THE AIR!

THEY DON'T DREAM OF LOOKING UP HERE IN THE SHADOWS!

THE YANKEE IS GONE! AND HE HAS BUILT US NO WEAPONS!

HE CANNOT BE FAR! FIND HIM AND DISPOSE OF HIM AS YOU DID THE OTHER WHO DARED DEFY ME!

THEY KILLED THE PROFESSOR-- A MAN WHO NEVER HARMED ANYONE IN HIS LIFE! THE MURDERING SWINE! THEY'LL PAY FOR IT! I SWEAR IT! IRON MAN SWEARS IT!

WHILE YOU HUNT DOWN YANKEE, I SHALL AMUSE MYSELF AT MY FAVORITE SPORT

THEN, SECONDS AFTER THE REDS DEPART...

YES, WONG-CHU, AMUSE YOURSELF WHILE YOU STILL CAN! FOR OUR MOMENT OF RECKONING IS ALMOST AT HAND!

YOU MAKE ME LOSE FACE! I **DESTROY** YOU!! EVEN **YOU** CAN BE SLAIN!

GUARDS-- OPEN FIRE!! DESTROY IRON MAN!

IT WILL TAKE MORE THAN SMALL ARMS FIRE TO PENETRATE MY CAST-IRON BODY!

PHANG **KAPOW!** **KAPOW!** **PAINNG**

GET GRENADES!! BRING **BAZOOKAS!!** QUICKLY, YOU FOOLS! QUICKLY!

BUT, BEFORE THE HEAVIER WEAPONS CAN BE BROUGHT INTO PLAY...

I'LL JUST REVERS THE CHARGE ON THIS MAGNETIC TURBO-INSULATOR.

...AND USE A TOP-HAT TRANSISTOR TO INCREASE ITS REPELLING POWER A THOUSANDFOLD!

STOP! COME **BACK!** THE MAGNET AFFECTS ONLY **METAL!** SHEER MAN-- POWER CAN **STILL** DEFEAT HIM!

THERE! REVERSE MAGNETISM -- IT WORKS LIKE A **CHARM!**

PANICKED BY THE INCREDIBLE DEMONSTRATION, THE GUERRILLA FLEE...

RUSHING INTO THE NEAREST BUILDING, WONG-CHU HEADS FOR THE STAIRS...

UPSTAIRS, THERE IS A LOUDSPEAKER! IN ALL THIS CONFUSION AND NOISE, THEY CAN-NOT HEAR ME! I MUST TALK OVER LOUD-SPEAKER!

LISTEN, MY WARRIORS! TEN THOUSAND YEN TO THE ONE WHO DESTROYS IRON MAN!

AWWKKK WWKKK BBBRRRK!

AN EASY MATTER FOR ME TO CREATE ELECTRICAL INTERFERENCE TO DROWN OUT HIS WORDS WITH STATIC!

AND THEN, TO FRUSTRATE THE WAR LORD'S EFFORTS EVEN FURTHER...

NOW I'LL SWITCH MY **OWN** VOICE ONTO THE LOUDSPEAKER!

DESERT WONG-CHU! FLEE INTO THE JUNGLE!

WHA--WHAT IS **HAPPENING??** THOSE NOT **MY** WORDS!

NONE CAN DEFEAT **IRON MAN!** FLEE, BEFORE HE SLAYS YOU ALL!!

IN PANIC, AND WITHOUT LEADERSHIP, THEY'LL SOON BE CAPTURED BY SOUTH VIETNAM TROOPS!

HE'S LOCKED THE DOOR BUT THAT WON'T KEEP **ME** OUT!

AND NOW TO SETTLE WITH WONG-CHU!

MY POWERFUL TRANSISTOR MAKES THIS MINIATURE BUZZ SAW INSIDE MY INDEX FINGER-CONTAINER OUT-PERFORM ANYTHING A DOZEN TIMES ITS SIZE!

ZZZZZZZZZ

ALL RIGHT, WAR LORD! YOU'RE **FINISHED!** COME DOWN HERE!

YOU MIGHT TERRIFY MY **TROOPS!** BUT NOT **WONG-CHU!**

TAKE **THIS,** MONSTER!

SMASH

NOW TO ORDER THE EXECUTION OF **ALL MY PRISONERS!**

-UGH!!- HE WEIGHTED EACH DRAWER OF THIS CABINET WITH ROCKS!

12

BUT NO DRAWERS FILLED WITH ROCKS CAN HOLD BACK IRON LIMBS POWERED BY ELECTRONIC TRANSISTORS!

KNOWING HE'S DEFEATED, WONG-CHU IS TRYING TO MURDER ALL HIS PRISONERS BEFORE HE'S STOPPED! I CANNOT ALLOW THAT!

I'M FREE! BUT IT TOOK ALMOST ALL MY ELECTRICAL POWER! I'VE GOT TO RECHARGE! I'M TOO LOW ON ENERGY TO PURSUE WONG-CHU!

YET, I CAN'T LET HIM GET AWAY! WAIT! I HAVE IT!

UNFASTENING HIS LUBRICATING APPARATUS, THE IRON MAN SQUIRTS OUT A THIN STREAM OF OIL...

I ESTIMATED IT JUST RIGHT! THE PRESSURE'S GREAT ENOUGH FOR IT TO REACH THE AMMO DUMP!

GUARDS! GUARDS! SLAY THE PRISONERS! NOW!

BARROOM

SECONDS LATER, IRON MAN HAS RECHARGED HIS BATTERIES, AND THEN...

I HAVE SET THE PRISONERS FREE, AND THE REDS HAVE FLED IN BLIND PANIC!

IT'S ALL OVER! NOW, PROFESSOR YINSEN, REST EASY! YOU, WHO SACRIFICED YOUR LIFE TO SAVE MINE, HAVE BEEN AVENGED!

AS FOR THE IRON MAN, THAT METALLIC HULK WHO ONCE WAS ANTHONY STARK... WHO KNOWS WHAT DESTINY AWAITS HIM? TIME ALONE WILL PROVIDE THE ANSWER! TIME ALONE...

THE END

DON'T MISS MORE OF IRON MAN IN THE NEXT GREAT ISSUE OF... TALES of SUSPENSE

That was then, and this is now!

Imagine how many changes have occurred in the life of Iron Man since that first, now-classic origin story.

Considering his wealth, fame and success, Tony Stark should be one of the happiest men in the world, right? No way!

In the drama-packed series which leads up to the tale you're about to thrill to, poor Tony had been riddled with guilt, due to the fact that some of the world's deadliest villains managed to steal the secret of his armored technology and were using it for their own evil purposes.

Feeling that he was to blame for the carnage that resulted, Tony Stark set out on a frantic, desperate quest, using all his wealth, all his power, to destroy every bit of his technology, regardless of whether it had fallen into the hands of friend or foe.

In his rage, Tony even dared challenge the might of the United States government itself! But the U.S. struck back, sending its own super-weapon to stop Iron Man. That weapon was the seemingly indestructible armored titan called "Firepower!"

In their final battle, unable to defeat the might Avenger any other way, Firepower launched a nuclear missile which shattered Iron Man's armor and seemed to mark "finish" to Tony Stark!

Now, in the aftermath that follows, we're about to witness a sensational turning point in the life of the invincible Iron Man!

So what are we waiting for? Let's go!

STAN LEE PRESENTS:
STARK WARS: CHAPTER 7
REBORN AGAIN

I'D LIKE TO BUY A VOWEL, PAT!

B-BUT, SKIPPER--!

--LATEST UPDATE ON THE RECENT TRAGEDY IN SOUTHERN CALIFORNIA.

IT WAS JUST DAYS AGO THAT THE WORLD SAW THE LAST OF--

--WHILE CITIZENS OF MANY COUNTRIES WERE SHOCKED--

--SOME WERE RELIEVED, EVEN GRATEFUL--

HERE'S THE STORY OF A MAN NAMED BRADY--

IT'S SAD TO SEE THE GREAT FALL SO FAR.

YES, TO BE FIRED FROM A COMPANY LIKE STARK ENTERPRISES--

--AND THEN KICKED OUT OF SUCH A PRESTIGIOUS ORGANIZATION AS THE AVENGERS--

GO, SPEED RACER, GO!

I WANNA ROCK FOR-EV-ERRRR!

THAT'S RIGHT, ED. THE MILITARY IS CONVINCED. IRON MAN IS DEFINITELY, ONE HUNDRED PER CENT--

INITIALLY, THE SOVIETS PROTESTED THE ABOVE-GROUND NUCLEAR DETONATION--

--BUT WHEN TOLD THE REASONS--

--DEAD!

83

WANT ME TO ROTATE THE *SATELLITE DISH,* CHIEF? SEE WHAT ELSE WE CAN GET?

NO, THANKS, *RHODEY.* I THINK WE'VE PICKED UP ALL THE *NEWS* WE'RE GOING TO. TO THE WORLD AT LARGE, MY ALTER EGO-- *IRON MAN*--IS IN THE GRAVE!

AND COME TO THINK OF IT, *I'M* NOT MUCH BETTER OFF!

THREE CRACKED RIBS, A SPRAINED ARM, A KNEE THAT MAY NEVER BE THE SAME.

TO SAY NOTHING OF A FACE THAT LOOKS LIKE IT WENT 40 ROUNDS WITH *ALI* IN HIS PRIME--

--AND SEVERAL PINTS OF SOMEONE ELSE'S AIDS-TESTED *BLOOD* RUNNING THROUGH MY VEINS!

C'MON, CHIEF, THE DOCS SAY YOUR RECUPERATION IS NOTHIN' SHORT OF *MIRACULOUS!* THOUGH THEY STILL DON'T KNOW HOW YOU COULDA GOT SO BANGED UP JUST FROM BEIN' THROWN OUTTA YOUR 'COPTER SEAT WHEN THAT NUKE WENT OFF!

THAT'S A LOT EASIER TO BELIEVE THAN THE *TRUTH,* BEGINNING WAY BACK WHEN *JUSTIN HAMMER* HAD *SPYMASTER* STEAL MY SECRET TECHNOLOGY!

THAT'S WHAT *STARTED* EVERYTHING, WHAT MADE ME GO AFTER ALL THE ARMORED TYPES HAMMER HAD SUPPLIED THOSE SECRETS *TO!*

FROM THE FIRST, I KNEW THERE'D BE A LOT OF PAIN-- AND NOT JUST *PHYSICAL* PAIN!

I CROSSED SO MANY LINES, WENT AGAINST FRIENDS, AGAINST COUNTRY.

I WANTED TO STOP MY TECHNOLOGY FROM CAUSING *HARM,* BUT TO THE PUBLIC IT LOOKED LIKE HARM WAS EXACTLY WHAT I WAS *CAUSING!*

"THAT'S WHY THE GOVERNMENT CAME AFTER ME WITH THE ULTIMATE FIGHTING MACHINE-- *FIREPOWER!*"

"AND HE BEAT THE LIVING CRAP OUT OF ME!"

"I TOOK REFUGE WITH YOU IN THE OBSERVATION 'COPTER, THINKING THE ARMY WOULD HOLD OFF THEIR ATTACK. I WAS *WRONG.*"

"SO IN DESPERATION, I HAD YOU EMPTY OUR STORES OF *WHOLE BLOOD* INTO MY POLARIZED ARMOR--"

"--THEN SENT THAT ARMOR OUT ON ITS OWN, CONTROLLING IT WITH TRANSMISSIONS FROM THE CHOPPER'S RADIO GEAR.

"FIREPOWER TOOK THE BAIT; MY ARMOR TOOK THE *NUKE!*"

AT LEAST *SOME* GOOD'S COME OF IT, THOUGH. PRESSURE'S EASING ON STARK ENTERPRISES, NOBODY'S HUNTIN' DOWN *IRON MAN* ANY MORE--

--AN' YOU'VE GOT A GREAT EXCUSE FOR BUILDIN' A NEW SUIT OF STATE-OF-THE-ART ARMOR!

NO, ALL OF MY RECENT TROUBLES WERE CAUSED BY THE *THEFT* OF DANGEROUS TECHNOLOGY I CREATED. AND I'M NOT GOING TO LET THAT HAPPEN *AGAIN.* TO EVERYONE BUT YOU AND ME, IRON MAN IS *DEAD.*

AND I'VE DECIDED TO *LEAVE* HIM THAT WAY!

FWACHAM

THANK YOU, PRIVATE BASKIN, CORPORAL WINTERS. YOUR *MARKSMANSHIP* WAS SUPERB!

HOW DID IT GO AT YOUR END, *JACK?*

NO KINKS, *MR. CORD.* STRUCTURAL INTEGRITY INTACT. SEEMS OUR LITTLE TUSSLE WITH IRON MAN DIDN'T DO THIS FIREPOWER ARMOR A *BIT* OF DAMAGE!

GOOD, GOOD, I'M GLAD TO HEAR -- AH. IT SEEMS WE HAVE *COMPANY.*

SENATOR BOYNTON! GENERAL MEADE! I'VE BEEN EXPECTING YOU!

I BELIEVE WE'VE GIVEN YOU AMPLE TIME TO RUN *FOLLOW-UP* TESTS ON THE FIREPOWER ARMOR, CORD.

IF YOU'LL HAVE *MR. TAGGERT* VACATE THE APPARATUS, WE'D LIKE TO TAKE CUSTODY NOW.

SORRY, BOYS, I'M NOT QUITE *THROUGH* WITH FIREPOWER YET!

WHAT?! NEED I REMIND YOU THAT THE GOVERNMENT *FINANCED* YOUR DEVELOPMENT OF FIREPOWER? WHY, WE'LL DRAG YOUR FANNY INTO *COURT* SO FAST--

FINE BY ME, SENATOR. OF COURSE, UNDER OATH I'D HAVE TO BE *HONEST*--

--TELL PEOPLE HOW FIREPOWER WASN'T REALLY CONCEIVED AS A WEAPON AGAINST *SUPER-HEROES*, BUT AS THE ULTIMATE IN *RIOT CONTROL!* TO BE USED AGAINST *CITIZENS* IN CASES OF EXTREME CIVIL DISORDER!

THE "*POST*" WOULD LOVE IT!

ER, P-PERHAPS I *WAS* A BIT HASTY--!

BULL COOKIES! THAT ARMOR'S GETTING ON THAT FLATBED TRUCK AND COMING WITH US!

SNAP

JACK?

SHABOWMM

FUNNY. *I* DON'T SEE ANY FLATBED TRUCK.

GOOD DAY, GENTLEMEN.

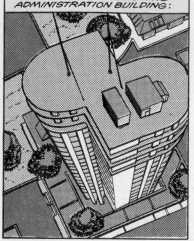

WHILE NORTH OF LOS ANGELES, A COMPANY HELICOPTER SETS DOWN ON THE GROUNDS OF *STARK ENTERPRISES*, AND TWO MEN WALK SLOWLY TOWARDS THE TOWERING ADMINISTRATION BUILDING:

PILOT *JAMES RHODES*, ALONG WITH FOUNDER AND C.E.O. *ANTHONY STARK*.

MR. STARK! UP AND AROUND SO SOON?

I'M GLAD YOU'RE BETTER, SIR!

I THINK I SPEAK FOR EVERYONE, MR. STARK, WHEN I SAY WE'RE *DELIGHTED* TO HAVE YOU BACK.

THANK YOU, MRS. ARBOGAST, AND TO CELEBRATE, I'D LIKE YOU TO SEND A MEMO TO ALL EMPLOYEES. QUOTE:

"THE DARK DAYS ARE OVER. WE'RE ON THE MOVE AGAIN!"

YES, SIR!

AS HEAD OF PUBLIC RELATIONS, MR. STARK, MIGHT I SUGGEST A NEW *CORPORATE SPOKESPERSON?* SOMEONE A BIT LESS *CONTROVERSIAL* THAN IRON MAN?

WHY DON'T I CONTACT *BILL COSBY'S* AGENT...?

BUT THOUGH TONY STARK HAS ANNOUNCED THAT DARK DAYS ARE OVER, *SOME* STORM CLOUDS LINGER STILL.

AS WITNESS AN EXECUTIVE MEETING THE FOLLOWING WEEK--

--AT THE *MARSTEN MANUFACTURING GROUP*...

NEVERTHELESS, THE CONTRACT BID FROM *STARK ENTERPRISES* IS LOWEST BY A CONSIDERABLE MARGIN. SO DESPITE THE RECENT TROUBLES THEY'VE HAD WITH *IRON MAN*, I RECOMMEND--

WAIT! Y-YOU CAN'T GO IN THERE--!

MS. CAMPBELL?! WHAT--?

I'M SORRY, SIR! BUT THIS MAN *INSISTS* ON ADDRESSING YOUR MEETING!

ACTUALLY--

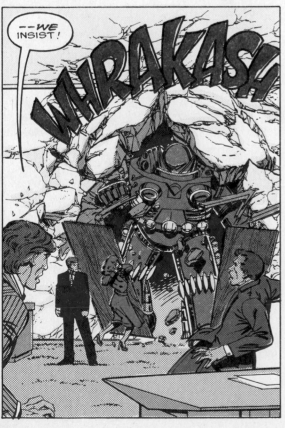

--WE INSIST!

WHRAKASH

NOW, ABOUT THAT *STARK* BID. I THINK IT WOULD BE HEALTHIER FOR ALL CONCERNED--

--IF YOU WERE TO TURN IT *DOWN!*

DAYS LATER--

ACCUTECH

LOADING BAYS

--ACCUTECH RESEARCH AND DEVELOPMENT--

--A SUBSIDIARY OF STARK ENTERPRISES--

WHABOOM

--EXPLODES!

TH-THAT FLYIN' GUY!

H-HE BLEW UP THE WHOLE SHIPMENT!

THAT'LL PUT US MONTHS BEHIND SCHEDULE!

AND EVENTUALLY, AFTER MORE DAYS AND MORE DESTRUCTION, AT THE STARK ENTERPRISES RAIL YARD...

SIR, I'VE CHECKED AND DOUBLE-CHECKED THIS SHIPMENT!

I KNOW, BILL. BUT I'LL FEEL A LITTLE BETTER TRIPLE-CHECKING IT MYSELF. WE CAN'T AFFORD TO LOSE ANOTHER ACCOUNT!

WITHOUT IRON MAN'S STIGMA TO WEIGH US DOWN, S.E.'S REVENUES SHOULD BE MOVING UPWARD--BUT THEY'RE FALLING INSTEAD!

AND ALL BECAUSE OF HARRASSMENT AND INTERFERENCE BY AN ARMORED WARRIOR WHO SOUNDS DISTURBINGLY LIKE--

--FIREPOWER!

SOMEONE'S STONEWALLING!

I FILED A FORMAL PROTEST IN WASHINGTON. THEY SAID THEY'D FORM A *COMMITTEE* TO LOOK INTO IT! WHAT A CROCK!

SO MUCH PRESSURE IS BEING APPLIED THAT I CAN'T EVEN GET THE *POLICE* TO DO ANYTHING! EVENTUALLY, THE SHEER *AUDACITY* OF ALL THIS WILL SPARK INTEREST; IF NOTHING ELSE, THE *PRESS* WILL INSIST ON KNOWING WHAT'S GOING ON.

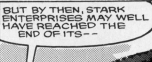

BUT BY THEN, STARK ENTERPRISES MAY WELL HAVE REACHED THE END OF ITS--

HEADS UP, CHIEF!

CHABOOM

INCOMING!

SSSHHHOOOF

OH, MY LORD! I-IT'S HIM!

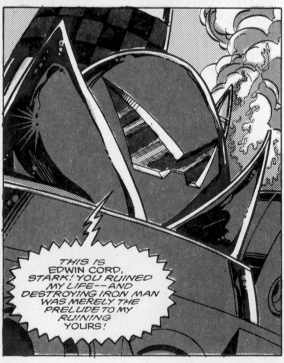

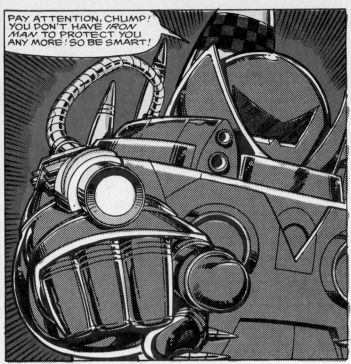

PAY ATTENTION, CHUMP! YOU DON'T HAVE *IRON MAN* TO PROTECT YOU ANY MORE! SO BE SMART!

DO WHAT YOU'RE *TOLD!*

SHROW

THAT GUY HURT US, CHIEF! HE HURT OUR *PEOPLE!* WHAT'S OUR NEXT MOVE?

I DON'T KNOW *YOU,* JIM, BUT AS FOR ME...

...I'M GOING HOME.

WHA--?!

CHIEF?

CHIEF?

IN THE WEEKS THAT FOLLOW, TONY STARK'S PACIFIC COAST MANSION BECOMES A WORLD OF ITS OWN, ISOLATED AND UNDISTURBED--

--WHERE THE ONLY SOUNDS ARE THE SCRITCHING OF A DRAFTING PENCIL, THE TACK-A-TACK OF COMPUTER KEYS, AND THE OCCASIONAL CURSE OF FRUSTRATION.

CALLING ON HONED SKILLS AND INNATE BRILLIANCE, THE MASTER OF THE MANSE FLESHES OUT IDEAS HE'S HAD FOR MONTHS, DEVISING AND REJECTING AND REVISING--

--AUGMENTING PROVEN COMPONENTS WITH NEW DISCOVERIES, SUCH AS A BETA PARTICLE POWER SUPPLY--

--AND INCLUDING EXPERIMENTAL ATTACK AND DEFENSE MODES WHOSE DANGERS AND ADVANTAGES CAN ONLY BE THEORIZED.

MOST IMPORTANTLY, HE CONSTRUCTS A SPECIAL SECURITY CHIP TO BE INCLUDED IN ALL PHASES OF DEVELOPMENT; ONE THAT WILL TRIGGER A SELF-DESTRUCT PULSE IF CIRCUIT DUPLICATION IS ATTEMPTED WITHOUT SECRET CODES THAT ONLY HE KNOWS--

THIS TECHNOLOGY WILL **NOT** BE USED BY OTHERS.

PHONES GO UNANSWERED. DOORBELLS RING UNHEEDED. FRIENDS BEGIN TO WONDER IF HE'S GONE OFF THE WAGON... OR WORSE, OVER THE EDGE.

BUT IN FACT, TOTAL SILENCE IS THE RESULT OF TOTAL CONCENTRATION; OF COMPLETE FOCUS ON AN ELUSIVE AND SOLITARY GOAL:

CREATION!

I KNOW THEY'RE *WORRIED* ABOUT ME--RHODEY, RAE, MRS. ARBOGAST AND THE REST. AND I WISH I COULD LET THEM IN ON THIS.

I'M *PROUD* OF WHAT I'VE *DONE.* THIS IS THE MOST *SOPHISTICATED,* MOST *ASTONISHING* INVENTION I'VE EVER CONSTRUCTED! BUT THAT'S THE PRECISE REASON--

--WHY IT HAS TO BE *DESTROYED!*

IT'S *TOO GOOD!* WITH ALL THE PAIN AND SORROW MY OTHER ARMOR CAUSED, I SHUDDER TO THINK WHAT COULD HAPPEN IF *THIS* FELL INTO EVIL HANDS.

EVEN *WITH* THE SECURITY CHIP!

I MAY BE A DREAMER, BUT I'M ALSO A *REALIST.* I KNOW I WON'T JUST ROLL OVER AND LET SOMEONE *TAKE* STARK ENTERPRISES. BUT AS SOON AS FIREPOWER IS DEALT WITH--

--I'M GOING TO *VAPORIZE* MY NEW ARMOR INTO *ATOMS!*

A BATTLE PLAN IS DEVISED. A LIKELY TARGET CHOSEN. AND SOME DAYS LATER, NORTH OF SAN FRANCISCO...

IT'S MY PLEASURE TO WELCOME THE NEWEST BRANCH OF *STARK ENTERPRISES* TO OUR COMMUNITY!

DESPITE RECENT *SETBACKS*, WE'RE SURE THIS FACILITY WILL BE AS GOOD FOR THE STARK ORGANIZATION AS IT WILL BE FOR THE WORK FORCE OF MARIN COUNTY!

WHAT IT'LL *BE*, CHUMP--

--IS THE WORST *MISTAKE* YOU EVER MADE!

CHAKOOM

YOU SHOULD KNOW BY NOW, COUNCILMAN, THAT PEOPLE WHO WORK FOR STARK RISK THEIR *HEALTH*--

--AND GROUPS THAT SUPPORT HIM RISK UTTER *DESTRUCTION*!

YOU MEAN, LIKE *THIS?*

SHRAK

NO! I--IT *CAN'T BE*--!

WISE UP, "CHUMP?" YOU MESS WITH MR. STARK'S INTERESTS, ANYWHERE IN THE *WORLD*, AND YOU'LL HAVE TO ANSWER TO--

--THE NEW IRON MAN!

STARK HIRED *ANOTHER* FOOL?

HE'S DUMBER'N I *THOUGHT*.

I'LL JUST ENGAGE MY TARGETING SYSTEM AND-- HUH? I--IT'S NOT *LOCKING!*

I STUDIED THE FIGHT YOU HAD WITH MY *PREDECESSOR*, AND I LEARNED A LOT!

INCLUDING HOW TO *JAM* YOUR *MISSILE-LOCK!*

I DON'T *NEED* IT!

HE'S FIRING A BARRAGE OF ROCKETS ANYWAY, AT RANDOM! TIME TO SEE HOW MY *RAPID-FIRE SEQUENCING* COMPUTER WORKS!

POOM *POOM*

POOM

POOM

EIGHT FOR EIGHT, IN THREE SECONDS! IF I SAY SO MYSELF--

--WOW!

NOW HE'S TURNING HIS *PARTICLE CANNONS* ON ME! BUT THE *ENERGY SHIELD* I CAN ACTIVATE FROM MY *LEFT GAUNTLET*, BASED ON ONE OF CORD'S *RAIDERS'* WEAPONS--

--IS ABSORBING THE CHARGE *PERFECTLY!*

MOVING AWAY? TRYING TO *REGROUP?* NOT IF MY REDESIGNED *PULSE BOLTS* CAN HELP IT!

UP CLOSE, THEY'RE NOT AS POWERFUL AS MY REPULSOR RAYS! BUT THEY KEEP PULSING, GAINING *STRENGTH,* THE FARTHER THEY GO! AND AT THIS DISTANCE, THEY SHOULD BE--

"-- DEVASTATING!"

CHAPRAK

I DIDN'T HAVE *THIS* MUCH TROUBLE IN MY *WHOLE* FIGHT WITH THE *OTHER* IRON MAN! MY ARMOR'S ACTUALLY *DAMAGED!* I'D BETTER GET OUT OF HERE BEFORE--

HUH? Y-YOU COVERED A HUNDRED YARDS IN A *SECOND?* H-HOW--?!

DID I FORGET TO MENTION THE IMPROVEMENTS MR. STARK MADE IN MY *BOOT PROPULSION SYSTEM?*

HOW CARE-LESS...!

WHAM

HAVE TO ACTIVATE ALL FUNCTIONING WEAPONS! THROW EVERYTHING I'VE *GOT* AT HIM! HE CAN'T DODGE IT *ALL!*

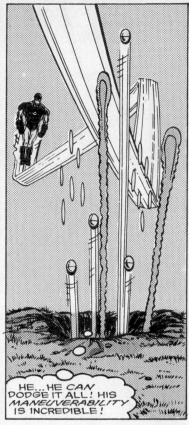

HE...HE *CAN* DODGE IT ALL! HIS *MANEUVERABILITY* IS INCREDIBLE!

BUT I STOPPED HIM *BEFORE*, AND I CAN STOP HIM *AGAIN!* THE SAME WAY!

WITH *TERMINAX!*

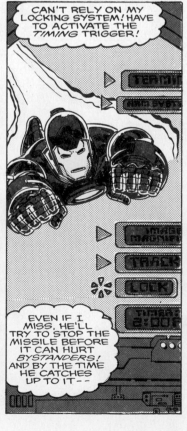

CAN'T RELY ON MY LOCKING SYSTEM! HAVE TO ACTIVATE THE *TIMING* TRIGGER!

TERMI...

ARM SYST...

IMAGE MAGNIF...

TRACK

LOCK

TIMER: 2:00...

EVEN IF I MISS, HE'LL TRY TO STOP THE MISSILE BEFORE IT CAN HURT *BYSTANDERS!* AND BY THE TIME HE CATCHES UP TO IT--

--IT'LL *EXPLODE!*

SO LONG, IRON MAN! GIVE MY REGARDS TO THE DE--

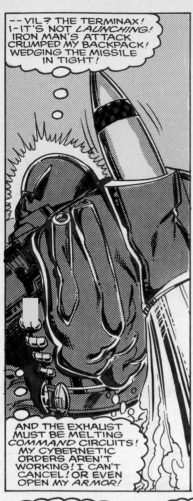

--YIL? THE TERMINAX! I-IT'S NOT *LAUNCHING!* IRON MAN'S ATTACK CRUMPED MY BACKPACK! WEDGING THE MISSILE IN TIGHT!

AND THE EXHAUST MUST BE MELTING *COMMAND* CIRCUITS! MY CYBERNETIC ORDERS AREN'T *WORKING!* I CAN'T *CANCEL!* OR EVEN OPEN *MY ARMOR!*

IRON MAN! THE NUKE'S ON A *TIMER!* A-AND I CAN'T *STOP* IT! GET ME *OUT* OF HERE!

SORRY, FIREPOWER, IF YOUR ARMOR'S *SEALED,* THERE'S NOTHING I CAN DO TO OPEN IT!

BUT YOU HAVE TO DO *SOMETHING!* WE'VE ONLY GOT THIRTY SECONDS!

THIRTY--?!

MY COMPUTERS COULD PROBABLY BREAK THE CANCELLATION CODE, BUT THAT'LL TAKE *TIME!*

I'LL HAVE TO *BUY* US SOME WITH AN *ELECTROMAGNETIC PULSE!* SOMETHING I LEARNED FROM *FORCE!* *

*IN ISSUE #224

THE *E.M.P.* CAN DAMPEN ELECTRICAL CIRCUITS FOR SIX MINUTES! UNFORTUNATELY, IT ALSO DRAINS *MY* POWER, ALL BUT MOBILITY AND LIFE SUPPORT, FOR THE SAME TIME! THAT MAKES ITS USES LIMITED, BUT IN THIS CASE IT MIGHT JUST--

WHAT HAPPENED?! MY READOUTS ARE DEAD! TH-THE TIMER'S *STOPPED!*

KEEP CALM! I'M GOING TO RUN A SENSOR SCAN!

PRECIOUS MINUTES CRAWL BY--

NEGATIVE
1 NEGATIVE
2 NEGATIVE
3 NEGATIVE
4 NEGATIVE
5 NEGATIVE
6 NEGATIVE
7 NEGATIVE
8 NEGATIVE
9 NEGATIVE

--AS THOUSANDS OF NUMERICAL COMBINATIONS ARE READ AND DISCARDED.

WHILE THE NEARBY CROWD WATCHES IN SILENCE, NOT FULLY AWARE OF THE AWESOME DANGER THEY'RE IN--

--NOR HOW LITTLE THEY COULD DO ABOUT IT EVEN IF THEY WERE.

IRON MAN! WH-WHATEVER YOU DID, IT'S WORN OFF! THE TIMER'S BACK ON!

WE'VE ONLY GOT NINE SECONDS!

HOLD STILL! I THINK I'VE FOUND THE CANCEL CODE! BUT I'LL HAVE TO USE A CYBER-PROBE TO MANIPULATE THE WARHEAD CIRCUITRY FROM OUTSIDE! TRY NOT TO BREATHE-- THIS IS RATHER DELICATE!

VERY DELICATE.

VERY DANGEROUS.

AND VERY...

KLIK

...SUCCESSFUL!

÷WHEW÷

TAKE IT EASY, FOLKS! EVERYTHING'S OKAY!

YOU THINK YOU'RE SMART, TIN MAN! BUT THERE'LL BE OTHERS! SOMEONE'LL KILL YOU--

--JUST LIKE I KILLED THE OTHER IRON MAN!

KRRRRIP

HUH?? Y-YOU MEAN, ALL THE TIME THAT *BOMB* WAS COUNTING DOWN, ALL THE TIME I WAS SWEATIN' MY *BUTT* OFF--

--YOU COULD'VE JUST TORN OFF MY *HELMET*?!

BUT YOU SAID YOU COULDN'T GET ME OUT!

I LIED.

THE SMALL SATISFACTION PASSES.

SIRENS WARBLE CLOSER.

IRON MAN DEPARTS.

FOR ALL TONY STARK WANTS NOW IS THE SANCTITY OF HIS COASTAL MANSION--

--AND THE SOLITUDE OF HIS WEARY THOUGHTS.

THERE'LL BE HUNDREDS OF QUESTIONS ABOUT THE NEW *IRON MAN,* AND I'LL HAVE TO ANSWER THEM ALL.

TOMORROW.

RIGHT NOW I NEED TO *REST,* TO REFLECT. I SWORE TO *DESTROY* MY NEW ARMOR, BUT WHAT FIREPOWER SAID WAS *TRUE*--THERE *WILL* BE OTHERS.

AND WHILE THEY MAY NOT ATTACK ME *DIRECTLY*, THERE ARE VERY FEW PEOPLE *POWERFUL* ENOUGH TO STAND AGAINST THEM, TO OFFER PROTECTION FOR THE BLAMELESS AND INNOCENT. AND WITH THIS ARMOR--

--I'M *ONE* OF THOSE FEW.

I DO HAVE A RESPONSIBILITY TO KEEP MY INVENTIONS FROM EVIL HANDS-- BUT I HAVE A *GREATER* RESPONSIBILITY TO *OPPOSE* THAT EVIL ANY WAY I CAN. SO... I GUESS *IRON MAN* WILL BE AROUND FOR A WHILE.

FUNNY. I STILL FEEL UNEASY, TROUBLED. BUT THE WAR IS *OVER*.

SLEEP. THAT'S WHAT I NEED.

YEAH.

THE FIRST GOOD NIGHT'S SLEEP--

--I'VE HAD IN AGES...!

THE *STARK WARS* SAGA WAS BROUGHT TO YOU BY :

DAVID MICHELINIE • DOC BRIGHT • BOB LAYTON • JANICE CHIANG • BOB SHAREN • MARK GRUENWALD • TOM DeFALCO
PLOT/SCRIPT • BREAKDOWNS • PLOT/FINISHES • LETTERS • COLORS • EDITOR • EDITOR IN CHIEF

PART THREE

IF YOU CAN'T BEAT 'EM, JOIN 'EM!

THE one thing we don't want you to do is worry. Therefore, we want you to know that Iron Man eventually defeated Whiplash. And, to make doubly certain that you don't dwell upon poor Tony Stark's never-ending tribulations, we've got another origins tale all lined up for you.

This time we'll be discussing a team once more. But not a team like the exemplary X-Men, which we created on a whim and tossed full-blown to the waiting world outside. No, the team we're now about to probe in depth consists of characters who had already become favorites amongst Marvelophiles everywhere. Two of them, The Incredible Hulk and The Mighty Thor, you've already met in the first volume of this sense-staggering series. The third member is Iron Man, whom we left just a scant few seconds ago. And that brings us to the fourth and fifth members of the group, Ant-Man and the wonderful Wasp.

Ah ha! I see your eyebrows slowly rising as you querulously mumble, "Hey, he never told us about any Ant-Man or any Wasp, wonderful or otherwise." Those of you who may not have been with Marvel during those fateful early days have a right to be mildly mystified. If you've come in late you may not recall the brief but brilliant career of Dr. Henry Pym and his lovely Jan. So settle back and relax as I try to fill the gap as best I can.

Though the Marvel Comics Group is known primarily for its world-famous, top-selling roster of superheroes, we've also published many other types of comicbooks throughout the years. Who among you does not feel his heart beat a bit faster at the very mention of our Western magazines, our romance titles, our humor books, our science-fiction masterpieces, our war stories, our sword-and-sorcery thrillers, our detective epics, our monster tales, and our ever-lovin' fantasy classics? Well, in 1962 we published one such fantasy strip called "The Man in the Ant-Hill," about a fella named Henry Pym who shrunk down to the size of an ant, to his everlasting consternation and regret. We featured that story on the cover of *Tales to Astonish* #27, just as we had featured hundreds of other stories on the covers of hundreds of other magazines. We never suspected that it would be anything special in any way, and promptly forgot all about it.

A short time later, when the sales figures were tabulated, we were amazed to find that the issue featuring "The Man in the Ant-Hill" had been one of our very best sellers for the entire year. Well, ain't no flies on Stan Lee! As soon as I learned that fateful fact I decided there must have been something about Henry Pym and his rather unusual habit of shrinking to ant size that had appealed to the minions of Marveldom. Armed with this conclusion, I took the very next step—I brought out a new strip named *Ant-Man*. Then, because no man is an island, I took the liberty of eventually giving the proper Mr. Pym a lady friend named Jan, who would ultimately be known as the wonderful Wasp.

However, despite what you may be thinking, despite any false clues I may have been dangling before you, this particular section of our tome does not deal with the origin of the Ant-Man strip. After all, we have to leave something for the subsequent volumes in this scholarly series. But, since The Ant-Man and his high-flying heroine appear in the saga which is soon to greet your hungry eyes, I just wanted to give you some background material. I never want you to feel as though you're reading about total strangers.

Let's see now, where were we? Oh yes, we're back in '63 again and it's time to concoct a brand-new superhero magazine. But this time, instead of making one up out of whole cloth, I decided to refer to our fan mail—because I suddenly remembered something. The mountain of fan mail we receive each day is one of the greatest things that's ever happened to us. From all over the country—in fact, from all over the free world, because our magazines are printed in virtually every part of the globe—we get tons of terrific letters from readers, telling us what we're doing right and, even more important, telling us what we're doing wrong. Through these exemplary epistles we're continually apprised of what you like about our books and what you loathe. We learn who your favorite heroes are, your favorite villains; we discover which artists you like best, which writers, editors, inkers, and letterers. By studying each and every letter, analyzing each and every comment, we can get a feeling of the type of stories you prefer, the type of situations that turn you on, and the type of plot lines we should develop. And now I'll get to the point.

I suddenly remembered that there had been one constant theme running through the fan mail for the past year or two. Most of our readers had been asking why we didn't take a few of our solitary, loner-type superheroes and let them join forces with some of our other heroes, thereby forming a superhero team. Fans were always asking things like, "Why don't The Human Torch and The Sub-Mariner join forces? Then we could have the power of fire combined with the power of water." Or "Why doesn't Spider-Man join with Daredevil since they both swing along the rooftops of New York?" Stuff like that.

Are you beginning to see the drift? Here I was trying to come up with a new superhero feature. I remembered all the mail requesting team-ups of our main characters. So what could be more logical than for me to act upon that very idea and do a new feature consisting of a group of our most dazzling do-gooders, united together in a common bond? Once again, in a frantic flurry of excitement, I called Jack Kirby and told him to sharpen his pencil.

Jack was the perfect choice for a team-type book, since he had drawn virtually all the characters I'd be wanting to use. As with all such projects, variety is one of the most necessary ingredients, so it was important to select a bevy of heroes who were all totally different. After kicking it around for a while, we came up with what seemed like a perfect combo. We'd start with The Hulk, just to make it difficult. Then, we'd include Thor, 'cause there's always room for a God of Thunder. Iron Man would be able to supply them all with weapons and bread whenever they needed it, and we'd toss in Ant-Man and the Wasp just for the sheer lunacy of it.

However, although it's easy enough to decide who the team should consist of, the tough part is figuring out how to get them all together. As you can imagine, it wouldn't make a terribly interesting story merely to have someone send the others a note inviting them to join a group of superheroes. We had to find a unique and exciting way of bringing this ill-assorted group together, and that meant introducing a villain who could be the catalyst. But what villain would be dangerous enough, powerful enough to have any effect on four of the most famous superheroes in the Marvel galaxy? The answer came to us in a blinding flash—Loki, God of Evil!

After talking it out a while longer, Jack and I were pretty much on top of the basic plot. And this time the title was a breeze to dream up. What better name could there be for a group of swingin' superheroes than—The Avengers? Now all we had to do was find lots of things for them to avenge, but that shouldn't be too hard. We had the team, and we had their name, and the rest should all be downhill!

Of course it takes more than a name and a bunch of characters to develop a series that will become best-sellers. It takes the fashioning of a world for the characters to live in, it takes a mood of realism to be created so that the reader feels he knows the characters, understands their problems, and cares about them. This would be injected in the issues that followed the origin you're about to read. We would dream up a headquarters for our glamorous little group, a mansion on the East Side of New York City, donated by multimillionaire Tony Stark. We even created a roster of new Avengers as time went by, additional members who were brought into the team—members like Captain America, Hawkeye, and The Vision. One of my favorite gimmicks was the little rallying cry I cooked up for them, the clarion call "Avengers Assemble!" which they'd shout in times of stress or danger, for no particular reason except that it looked so zingy when it was lettered real large at the top of the panel!

But all these things we've mentioned came later on, in subsequent issues, as the series kept growing and developing. Right now, it's back to basics for us. Right now, through the miracle of our imaginations, we're back in the year 1963. We walk up to a newsstand and there, before our startled eyes, we see the first fabulous cover of a brand new comicbook called *The Avengers*. Tremulously our collective hand reaches out, gallantly clutching a dime and two pennies. Eagerly, our valiant hearts beating in breathless anticipation, we grasp the brightly colored treasure as we slowly flip the phantasmagoric pages, all but hypnotized by the wonderment within.

Just think, you lucky devil, all of that pleasure is now about to be yours. . . .

"THE COMING OF THE AVENGERS!

THE FIRST OF A STAR-STUDDED SERIES of **BOOK-LENGTH SUPER-EPICS** *featuring some of* EARTH'S GREATEST SUPER-HEROES!

THE MIGHTY THOR

IRON-MAN

ANT-MAN and the WASP

THE PLACE: ASGARD, HOME OF THE NORSE GODS!

THE TIME: THE PRESENT!

THE MAN: LOKI, GOD OF EVIL! A PRISONER ON THE DREADED *ISLE OF SILENCE*...PLOTTING AWESOME REVENGE AGAINST HIS MIGHTY ENEMY, THOR, THE THUNDER GOD!

| WRITTEN BY: STAN LEE | DRAWN BY: JACK KIRBY | INKING: DICK AYERS | LETTERING: S. ROSEN |

The Incredible HULK

IT IS BECAUSE OF THE ACCURSED **THOR** THAT I AM EXILED TO THIS BARREN ISLE, ORDERED TO **REMAIN** HERE BY **ODIN**, KING OF THE GODS!

BUT THOUGH MY **BODY** MAY BE IMPRISONED, **NONE** CAN STOP MY MAGIC **POWERS** FROM ROAMING THE UNIVERSE IN SEARCH OF **REVENGE!**

BY MEANS OF **THOUGHT PROJECTION** I SHALL SEND MY DISEMBODIED SELF PAST THE RAINBOW BRIDGE DOWN TO EARTH! THERE I SHALL FIND SOME WAY TO MAKE **THOR** COME BACK TO ASGARD, WHERE I CAN BATTLE HIM AGAIN, AND **DEFEAT** HIM FOREVER!

THERE HE IS, IN HIS HUMAN IDENTITY AS **DR. DON BLAKE**, LAME, MILD-MANNERED TREATER OF THE SICK AND INJURED!

S'LONG, DOC! I FEEL LOTS BETTER NOW!

HIT A FEW HOMERS IN TODAY'S GAME FOR ME, BOBBY!

BAH! DEFEATING DON BLAKE MEANS **NOTHING** TO ME! IT WOULD BE A HOLLOW VICTORY!

ONLY BY CONQUERING HIM AS **THOR** WILL MY REVENGE BE COMPLETE! BUT IT WILL REQUIRE A FEARFUL MENACE TO MAKE THE DULL DOCTOR BECOME THE MIGHTY THUNDER GOD! I MUST SCAN EARTH TILL I **FIND** SUCH A MENACE!

After LONG HOURS OF SUPER-NATURAL OBSERVATION, **LOKI** FINDS...

A HUGE HUMAN FIGURE... FLYING THROUGH THE AIR! HOW IS IT POSSIBLE?

NO...HE IS **NOT** FLYING! HE IS COVERING THE AREA IN FANTASTIC, POWERFUL **LEAPS!** NOW I SEE! IT IS THE INCREDIBLE **HULK!!**

2.

ALTHOUGH THERE IS NO EVIL IN HIS HEART, MANKIND *FEARS* HIM BECAUSE OF HIS AWESOME STRENGTH! *HE* SHALL BE THE PERFECT FOIL FOR ME!

BUT, WHAT DIABOLICAL SCHEME SHALL I EMPLOY? AH, I HAVE IT! THAT *RAILROAD TRESTLE!*

ALL I NEED DO IS PROJECT A MENTAL IMAGE UPON THE TRACKS, WHERE THE *HULK* WILL SEE IT!

THERE, IT IS DONE! THE WITLESS MORTAL WILL THINK HE SEES A REAL BUNDLE OF TNT, ABOUT TO DESTROY THE TRESTLE JUST AS THE TRAIN IS APPROACHING!

PERFECT! HE *SEES* IT! AND NOW, NOT DREAMING IT IS ONLY A NON-EXISTENT IMAGE, HE LEAPS DOWN TO SNUFF IT OUT BEFORE IT CAN EXPLODE!

BUT THERE IS *NO* TNT, AND SO, REACHING FOR SOMETHING THAT IS NOT THERE, HE MISCALCULATES THE FORCE OF HIS PLUNGE, CRASHING INTO THE TRESTLE, AND *SHATTERING* IT!

CHARLIE! STOP THE TRAIN! SOMETHING SMASHED THE TRESTLE UP AHEAD! WE'LL CRASH!

IMPOSSIBLE!! WE'RE GOING TOO FAST! WE'LL *NEVER* STOP IN TIME!

HAH! IT WORKED JUST AS I PLANNED! WHEN THE TRAIN CRASHES, THE *HULK* WILL BE BLAMED! HE WILL BECOME THE MOST WANTED MAN ON EARTH! DR. BLAKE IS CERTAIN TO BECOME *THOR* TO JOIN IN THE HUNT...LITTLE DREAMING THAT THAT IS JUST WHAT *LOKI* WANTS! BUT, *WAIT!* WHY IS THE *HULK* CARRYING THAT HUGE BOULDER?

HE HAS PLACED IT UNDER THE TRACKS!...IS USING IT AS A SUPPORT, TO STAND ON! THE *FOOL!* WHAT GOOD WILL *THAT* DO? THE TRAIN IS ALMOST UPON HIM!

LOOK! THAT HEAD JUTTING THROUGH THE TRACKS!

IT'S THE HULK! HE DID THIS! HE'S TRYING TO KILL US ALL! I--I CAN'T STOP IN TIME!

BUT, USING THE ALMOST LIMITLESS STRENGTH OF HIS INCREDIBLE BODY, THE **HULK** BENDS BELOW THE TRACKS, SUPPORTING THEM WITH HIS MASSIVE BACK, AS THE TRAIN PASSES SAFELY BY...

BUT THEN...

ALL SAFE! ..CAN'T HOLD ANY LONGER...

WHOOSH!

CRASH!

HE SAVED THE TRAIN, BUT ONLY I KNOW THAT! THE HUMANS WILL STILL THINK HE TRIED TO SLAY THEM...THE HUNT WILL BE ON! AND **THOR** WILL LIVE AGAIN!...ALL BECAUSE OF **LOKI,** THE MASTER SCHEMER!

HOURS LATER, AS LOKI PREDICTED...

BETTER LOCK YOUR DOORS, BOYS! THE **HULK'S** ON THE RAMPAGE AGAIN!

A LOT OF GOOD LOCKING A DOOR WILL DO AGAINST **THAT** GORILLA!

CITY NEWS

HULK IN ATTACK ON TRAIN! NATION SHOCKED! ARMY TO MOBILIZE!

THEN, THE ONE LIVING BEING WHO KNOWS THE TRUTH ABOUT THE **HULK** READS THE REPORT IN AMAZEMENT!

IT **CAN'T** BE! HE'D **NEVER** DO A THING LIKE THAT!..NO MATTER **WHAT!!**

OR..OR **WOULD** HE?

CITY NEWS

TRAIN ENGINEER IDENTIFIES HULK AS WOULD-BE WRECKER!

CITY

HUL IN ATT ON TRA

WITHIN MINUTES, **RICK JONES** SUMMONS MEMBERS OF HIS NEWLY FORMED **TEEN BRIGADE***, A GROUP OF YOUTHFUL RADIO HAM ENTHUSIASTS...

IF THE **HULK** IS INNOCENT, HE NEEDS HELP, FAST! AND IF HE'S GUILTY, IT'LL TAKE MORE THAN THE **ARMY** TO STOP 'IM!

WE'VE GOTTA CONTACT SOMEONE WITH EQUAL POWERS...LIKE THE **FANTASTIC FOUR!**

TEEN BRIGADE FORMED IN ISSUE OF HULK #6.

DON'T JUST SIT THERE, FELLA! START SENDING! USE THE FF'S SPECIAL WAVELENGTH! TELL 'EM TO CONTACT ME, **PRONTO,** BEFORE ANY INNOCENT JOKERS GET HURT REAL BAD!

YOU HEARD THE MAN, WILLIE! NOW **MOVE!**

AND SO, SECONDS LATER, A FRANTIC MESSAGE IS BEAMED FROM THE HEADQUARTERS OF THE **TEEN BRIGADE,** IN THE SOUTHWEST, HALFWAY ACROSS THE COUNTRY TOWARDS NEW YORK!

CALLING THE **FANTASTIC FOUR!** CONDITION **RED!** CONTACT **TEEN BRIGADE!! HULK** MUST BE FOUND!! DO YOU READ ME?

4.

BUT THE SINISTER GOD OF EVIL HAS *OTHER* PLANS...

THE *FANTASTIC FOUR* WILL RUIN EVERYTHING! IT IS *THOR* I WANT!...NO ONE ELSE! I MUST TAKE INSTANT ACTION!

THERE! I HAVE USED MY *MENTAL POWERS* TO JAM THE RADIO WAVES, DIVERTING THEM TO A DIFFERENT WAVE-LENGTH...ONE WHICH I KNOW *DON BLAKE* IS LISTENING TO!

AND, IN THE QUIET STUDY OF DR. BLAKE...

...CONTACT *TEEN BRIGADE!* HULK MUST BE FOUND! DO YOU READ US?

STRANGE! SOUNDS LIKE A CALL FOR *THOR!*

THE *TEEN BRIGADE!* THEY'RE LOCATED IN THE SOUTH-WEST! IF THIS CONCERNS THE *HULK,* IT MUST BE SERIOUS! AND SO, THE TIME HAS COME...

...FOR DR. DON BLAKE TO STRIKE HIS ENCHANTED CANE ONCE UPON THE FLOOR, CASTING OFF HIS MORTAL GUISE, AND BECOMING...

...THE MIGHTY *THOR,* GOD OF *THUNDER!*

BUT, UNSUSPECTED BY *LOKI,* OTHERS HAVE *ALSO* HEARD THE RADIO MESSAGE, AND THOUGHT IT WAS BEAMED TO THEM! AMONG THEM ARE THE ASTONISHING *ANT-MAN* AND THE *WASP!*

WAIT FOR *ME, ANT-MAN!*

I THOUGHT YOU WEREN'T COMING, JAN!

I CAN'T SEE WHY YOU HAVE TO STOP AND POWDER YOUR NOSE EVERY TIME WE HAVE A MISSION!

HENRY PYM, YOU'RE BEGIN-NING TO SOUND LIKE A STUFFY OLD *BACHELOR* AGAIN!

AND I INTEND TO *REMAIN* THAT WAY! NOW SEE IF YOU CAN'T BE QUIET LONG ENOUGH FOR ME TO ACTIVATE THE DOUBLE CATAPULT!

BUT WHY DO *I* HAVE TO USE YOUR *SILLY FLYING ANT RELAYS?* I HAPPEN TO HAVE *MY OWN* WINGS!

BUT WE'VE GOT A *THOUSAND* MILES TO COVER, JAN, AND I DON'T WANT YOU EXHAUSTED WHEN WE GET THERE!

AND STILL **ANOTHER** PAIR OF EARS HAVE INTERCEPTED THE URGENT BROADCAST...THE EARS OF **ANTHONY STARK**, MILLIONAIRE INDUSTRIALIST AND PLAYBOY...BETTER KNOWN TO THE UNSUSPECTING WORLD AS **IRON MAN!**

LUCKY I WAS TUNED IN TO THE RIGHT FREQUENCY! THINGS HAVE BEEN TOO DULL AROUND HERE LATELY!

I'VE ALWAYS **WONDERED** WHETHER THE **HULK** REALLY EXISTED, AND WHETHER **IRON MAN'S** STRENGTH WAS A MATCH FOR HIM!

LOOKS AS THOUGH I'LL GET A CHANCE TO FIND OUT! SOONER THAN I THOUGHT!

I'LL PROPEL MYSELF FOR MOST OF THE TRIP BY MY SOLAR BATTERY! IT'S SLOWER THAN MY TRANSISTORS, BUT IT LASTS LONGER...AND I'VE GOT A LONG WAY TO GO!

THEN, AFTER A FEW HOURS OF CROSS-COUNTRY FLYING...

ALMOST THERE! NOW TO SWITCH TO MY TRANSISTORS BEFORE I LULL MYSELF TO SLEEP UP HERE!

AHHH! THIS IS MORE **LIKE** IT!

MEANWHILE, IN THE MAIN CLUBROOM OF THE **TEEN BRIGADE**, A FEELING OF **GLOOM** FILLS THE AIR...

STILL NO WORD FROM THE FF, EH?

GUESS THEY NEVER GOT THE MESSAGE!

OR ELSE THEY CAN'T BE BOTHERED TO ANSWER A BUNCH OF KIDS LIKE US!

HEY! HOLD IT, YOU GUYS! **CLAM UP!** I'M GETTIN' SOMETHIN'...IT..IT'S **MR. FANTASTIC!**

WELL, C'MON, RICK... **GIVE!!** WHAT DOES HE **SAY?** LET US IN ON IT!!

WE'VE JUST INTERCEPTED A MESSAGE FROM YOU, RICK! IT WAS BROADCAST ON THE WRONG WAVELENGTH SOMEHOW!

PHOOEY! EVERYTIME THERE'S SOMETHIN' HEAVY TO BE LIFTED AROUND HERE, OL' PRETTY BOY GETS A CALL ON THAT BLASTED RADIO!

BEN GRIMM! YOU KNOW YOU GET MIKE FRIGHT EVERY TIME **YOU** HAVE TO USE IT!

6.

WE'RE WRAPPED UP IN ANOTHER CASE NOW, SON, BUT...

..ACCORDING TO MY CALCULATIONS, YOUR MESSAGE SHOULD BE PICKED UP BY SOME *OTHERS* WHO CAN HELP YOU! IF YOU DON'T GET HELP SOON, RADIO BACK AND LET ME KNOW!

YOU *KIDDIN'*, REED? WHO *ELSE* COULD EVER DO WHAT *WE* CAN DO?

THEN, AS THE CONTACT IS BROKEN, AS IF IN ANSWER TO THE *HUMAN TORCH'S* BANTERING QUESTION ---

LOOKS LIKE WE STRUCK OUT, RICK! THE FF CAN'T MAKE IT, HUH?

WONDER WHAT HE MEANT ABOUT SOMEONE *ELSE* MAYBE HELPIN' US?

AW, JUST SOME BUCK-PASSIN'! THAT'S ALL!

H-HEY, GUYS... *LOOK!*

WHY SO *SURPRISED?* DIDN'T YOU *SEND* FOR ME?

WOWEE! IT'S *THOR!!*

LOOK! FLYIN' ABOVE US! IT'S *ANT-MAN* AND *THE WASP!*

IT WOULD SEEM AS THOUGH THE GANG'S ALL HERE, EH, LADS?

HENRY! DID YOU SEE THAT *GORGEOUS* THOR?! HOW CAN I EVER MAKE HIM NOTICE ME?

STOP ACTING LIKE A LOVESICK FEMALE AND SLIP BEHIND THIS LENS WITH ME! I'LL ADJUST IT SO IT'LL PROJECT OUR IMAGES ON THE WALL!

WE HEARD THAT YOU NEEDED HELP, BOYS! IT CERTAINLY LOOKS AS THOUGH YOU'RE GOING TO *GET* IT!

THIS IS THE *COOLEST!* FIRST *THOR*, THEN *IRON MAN*, AND NOW *ANT-MAN* AND THE *WASP!* IT'S MORE THAN WE DARED *HOPE* FOR!

7.

BUT, BACK IN ASGARD...

BAH! THIS COMPLICATES THINGS FOR ME! I ONLY WANT TO FIND A WAY TO LURE THOR UP HERE! I AM NOT INTERESTED IN THOSE OTHERS!

THOR IS AT THE WINDOW NOW! IF I MOVE QUICKLY, I MAY STILL SUCCEED! I'LL CREATE A MENTAL IMAGE OF THE HULK AND MAKE IT RUN PAST THOR'S FIELD OF VISION!

I THOUGHT I SAW... IT IS! IT'S THE HULK!

NO NEED FOR ME TO DISTURB THE OTHERS!

NO MATTER HOW FAST HE CAN LEAP, I CAN ALWAYS FOLLOW HIM!...

...BY HURLING MY MIGHTY HAMMER AND HOLDING ONTO THE UNBREAKABLE THONG!

STRANGE! HE MOVES AS THOUGH HE HASN'T SEEN ME...AS THOUGH HE IS UNAWARE OF ANYTHING!

NO! NOW HE SEES ME! HE IS GRASPING THAT HUGE BOULDER! HE INTENDS TO HURL IT AT ME! BUT MY HAMMER WILL STOP HIM!

IMPOSSIBLE! IT... IT WENT RIGHT THROUGH HIM!

NOW HE'S FADING AWAY! IT ISN'T THE HULK AT ALL! MERELY A MENTAL IMAGE!

ONLY LOKI IS CAPABLE OF SUCH WIZARDRY! I SHOULD HAVE SUSPECTED! HE MUST BE BEHIND IT!

8.

LOKI, THOU EVIL ONE! I KNOW NOT WHAT YOUR PLAN IS, BUT I HAVE *WARNED* YOU NEVER TO MEDDLE IN EARTH AFFAIRS! AND NOW YOU DARE DEFY ME!

I HAVE *SUCCEEDED!* HE IS RETURNING TO ASGARD! BUT WHEN HE REACHES THE ISLE OF SILENCE, IT IS *I* WHO SHALL EMERGE THE *VICTOR!*...FOR THIS TIME I AM *READY* FOR THE COMING OF *THOR!*

BUT, BACK ON EARTH, THE WHEELS SET IN MOTION BY VILLAINOUS *LOKI* CANNOT BE STOPPED! THE *HULK* IS STILL AT LARGE... AND OUR AMAZING SAGA HAS BARELY BEGUN!

THOR HAS DISAPPEARED! BUT DON'T WORRY, LAD!... I'M SURE THAT *ANT-MAN* AND I WILL BE ABLE TO FIND THE *HULK* AND TO LEARN THE TRUTH!

IF HE REALLY *IS* ON A RAMPAGE, LOOK OUT!! HE'S STRONGER THAN ANYONE EVEN *SUSPECTS!* BUT IF HE'S INNOCENT, HE MUST NOT BE HURT... UNDERSTAND?

MEANWHILE, WHERE *IS* THE INCREDIBLE *HULK?* HUNTED, HOUNDED, BEWILDERED, HE HAS TAKEN REFUGE WITH A TRAVELING CIRCUS, AS HE WONDERS WHAT TO DO NEXT!

THERE HE *IS* LADIES AND GENTLEMEN... *MECHANO*, THE MOST POWERFUL, LIFELIKE ROBOT ON EARTH! HE WALKS LIKE A MAN, HE MOVES LIKE A MAN, BUT HE IS AS STRONG AS A DOZEN BULLDOZERS! *MECHANO*, THE MARVEL OF THE AGE!!

I'M TRAPPED IN THIS CREVICE! CAN'T BE AN ACCIDENT! SOMEONE MUST BE WISE TO ME! DON'T KNOW HOW THEY DID IT, BUT THAT'S NOT IMPORTANT NOW! CAN'T STAY HERE... GOTTA GET OUT!

EXERTING HIS INCREDIBLY POWERFUL MUSCLES TO FULL CAPACITY, THE MADDENED HULK THRASHES AND POUNDS AND BATTERS AND HEAVES, UNTIL...

THERE'S NOT A PIECE OF GROUND ANYWHERE THAT CAN HOLD THE HULK!

I'M FREE!!

I FLEW CLOSE ENOUGH TO BE SURE...IT IS HIM...IT'S THE HULK!

WHAT'S THAT FLYIN' PAST ME?? JUST A COUPLE OF BUGS! NO...THEY..THEY LOOK LIKE PEOPLE!

I DON'T GET THIS!...BUT I DON'T LIKE WHAT I SEE! GOTTA LEAVE HERE! THEY'RE STARTIN' TO CLOSE IN!

I'LL USE THE MICROPHONE TO MAKE HIM HEAR ME! MAYBE I CAN REASON WITH HIM!

I SURE WOULDN'T WANT TO MEET HIM IN A DARK ALLEY...OR EVEN A LIGHT ONE!

WAIT! THIS IS ANT MAN TALKING! I KNOW WHO YOU ARE! I MUST SPEAK TO YOU! IF YOU'RE INNOCENT, I'LL HELP YOU! I'M YOUR FRIEND!

GO AWAY! I SPEAK TO NO ONE! I HAVE NO FRIENDS!

IF YOU WON'T STOP, I'LL MAKE YOU STOP! RELEASE THE STEEL CYLINDER, MY TINY WARRIORS!

YOU ARE A FOOL! NOTHING CAN STOP ME!

DON'T BE TOO SURE OF THAT!

OOOFF!

MEANWHILE, THE AUDIENCE, THINKING IT IS ALL PART OF THE SHOW, HOWLS WITH UNRESTRAINED ENTHUSIASM...

BEST DURN ACT I EVER SAW!

THAT BIG ROBOT HAS THE DISPOSITION OF MY BROTHER-IN-LAW!

HOW DO THEY EVER DREAM THESE THINGS UP?

SO! YOU REFUSE TO STOP??

YOU INTEND TO KEEP HOUNDING ME, DO YOU?

ALL RIGHT, THE MASQUERADE'S OVER! I DON'T CARE WHO KNOWS WHO I AM! SOON AS I WIPE THIS STUPID MAKE-UP OFF, I'M GONNA RIP THIS PLACE APART WITH MY BARE HANDS! WHAT HAVE I GOT TO FEAR! NOTHING CAN HURT THE HULK!

THEN, AS THE STARTLED, INCREDULOUS AUDIENCE RECOILS IN PANIC...

WE'VE DONE IT! WE'VE BROUGHT HIM OUT INTO THE OPEN! NOW EVERY SECOND COUNTS! LURE HIM UNDER THE TRAPEZE NET! I'LL DO THE REST!

DON'T LET ME DOWN, HENRY! I WOULDN'T WANT HIM FOR A PERMANENT PLAYMATE!

THE INSECT-WOMAN AGAIN! WHY DO YOU BUZZ AROUND ME?? YOU MUST BE AN ENEMY! I CAN FEEL IT!

HOW CAN ANY-ONE SO BIG MOVE SO FAST? HE'S THE MOST DREADFUL THING I'VE EVER SEEN!

YOU THINK YOU CAN ESCAPE ME BECAUSE OF YOUR SIZE? NO ONE ESCAPES THE HULK!

OHHH...

THAT BELLOWS! FEELS LIKE A HURRICANE! ≤GASP!≤ CAN'T BREATHE! CAN'T SEE...OUT OF CONTROL! HENRY... HELP!!

NO ONE CAN SAVE YOU NOW!

12.

SUDDENLY, A MASSIVE GOLDEN FIGURE BREAKS THROUGH THE CROWD OF AMAZED SPECTATORS, AND THE SHOCK OF SEEING *IRON MAN* CHARGING TOWARDS HIM MAKES THE *HULK* TEMPORARILY FORGET HIS TINY PRISONER!

YOU'RE **WRONG!** THERE IS **ONE** WHO CAN SAVE HER!

IRON MAN!

THROUGH HIS TRANSISTOR-POWERED, BUILT-IN RADIO RECEIVER, THE GOLDEN WARRIOR HEARS A TERSE REPORT FROM NEARBY *ANT-MAN!*

PERFECT TIMING, *IRON MAN!* NOW, QUICKLY... MAKE HIM RUN TOWARD THE CENTER OF THE ARENA! I'VE PREPARED A TRAP FOR HIM! LET HIM TRY TO ESCAPE BY LEAPING THROUGH THE TOP OF THE TENT!

AND, AS THE *HULK* EXECUTES ONE OF HIS INCREDIBLE LEAPS, CRASHING THROUGH THE VERY TOP OF THE CIRCUS TENT...

ARGHH!

HE HIT THE SPECIAL NYLON SAFETY NETTING WHICH MY ANTS SPREAD OVER THE TOP OF THE TENT! NOW IF IT WILL ONLY HOLD HIM LONG ENOUGH!

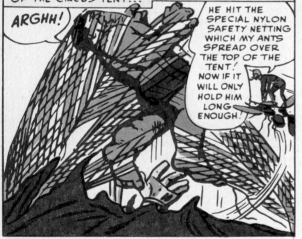

BUT CAN ANY MERE NYLON NETTING BE STRONG ENOUGH TO HOLD THE RAMPAGING, EXPLODING HUMAN POWERHOUSE THAT IS THE *HULK?* WITH A MIGHTY SURGE OF BRUTE FORCE HE HURLS HIMSELF UPWARD, TAKING ALL THE NETTING AND THE ENTIRE TENT WITH HIM!

HE'S GETTING **AWAY!!**

NEVER HAVE HUMAN EYES BEHELD SUCH AN AWESOME SPECTACLE... NEVER HAS MORTAL MAN WITNESSED SUCH A STUPENDOUS SIGHT!!

SECONDS LATER, HAVING RIPPED OFF THE ENTANGLING FABRICS ON THE SHAGGY PEAKS NEARBY, THE *HULK* CONTINUES HIS FRENZIED FLIGHT... WITH A LONE PURSUER!

THERE IS NO PLACE ON EARTH WHERE I CANNOT FOLLOW YOU!

13.

SUDDENLY, THE MIGHTY FUGITIVE DROPS TO EARTH, AS HIS GOLDEN PURSUER, UNABLE TO STOP IN TIME, WHIZZES OVER HIM!

THEN, WITH THE SPEED OF A CHARGING DREADNOUGHT, THE *HULK* LEAPS INTO THE AIR AGAIN, BEHIND THE STARTLED *IRON MAN!*

IN A TRICE THE HUNTED HAS BECOME THE HUNTER, AS A THUNDEROUS BLOW TO HIS POWER-PACK DAMAGES *IRON MAN'S* PROPULSION BATTERY!

NO ONE CAN STOP THE *HULK!*

CAN'T GO AFTER HIM TILL I REPAIR MY BATTERY!

HULK... WAIT! I WANT TO *HELP* YOU! TRUST ME! YOU CAN'T REMAIN A FUGITIVE *FOREVER!* COME BACK!!

BAH! I DON'T TRUST *ANYBODY!*

MEANWHILE, WHAT OF THE MIGHTY *THOR?* AT THAT MOMENT, IN THE GRAND CHAMBER OF THE IMPERIAL PALACE AT ASGARD...

NOBLE ODIN, LORD OF GODS! GRANT THY SON PERMISSION TO VISIT *LOKI* ON THE ISLE OF SILENCE, THAT I MAY LEARN IF HE IS RESPONSIBLE FOR SOME DEVILTRY ON EARTH!

WE GRANT THEE PERMISSION, BELOVED *THOR!* BUT HARK TO THESE WORDS...

THOUGH *YOU* BE THE SON OF MY HEART..*LOKI* TOO IS MY SON! I CANNOT INTERFERE IN WHAT TRANSPIRES BETWEEN YOU!

I UNDERSTAND, FATHER!

AND SO, ALONE IN THE NIGHT, THE MIGHTY THUNDER-GOD SETS OUT ACROSS THE SEA OF MIST... AWARE THAT THE ENEMY HE SEEKS IS ALSO A LEGENDARY GOD...AND THE MOST SINISTER, THE MOST DANGEROUS OF ALL!

LOKI MUST KNOW I AM COMING! HE MUST HAVE SET MANY TRAPS FOR ME! BUT I DARE NOT TURN BACK ...NO MATTER WHAT THE RISK!

14.

THE ISLE IS DIRECTLY AHEAD! LUCKILY MY LUNGS ARE STRONG... IF I CAN JUST HOLD MY BREATH FOR ANOTHER FEW MINUTES!

AND, ON SHORE, A GLOATING FIGURE SURVEYS THE NOW-SILENT SEA...

HIS CRAFT IS EMPTY! HE IS NOWHERE TO BE SEEN! HAVE I DEFEATED HIM SO SOON?!

THEN, AS IF IN ANSWER TO LOKI'S WORDS, A GIGANTIC WATER-SPOUT SHOOTS INTO THE AIR... AND...

NO, EVIL BROTHER! THE BATTLE HAS YET TO BEGIN!

HAVE YOU FORGOTTEN MY HAMMER IS CAPABLE OF CREATING WATER-SPOUTS, AS WELL AS PUNISHING MY FOES!?

WITH THE SPEED OF THOUGHT, LOKI FREEZES THE MOLECULES IN THE AIR, CREATING AN ICY SHIELD, JUST STRONG ENOUGH TO DEFLECT THOR'S HAMMER!

HAH! I AM TOO FAST FOR YOU!

YOU WERE EXPECTING ME, LOKI! THAT MEANS YOU HAVE COMMITTED SOME FOUL DEED, KNOWING I WOULD COME TO AVENGE IT!

AND AVENGE IT I SHALL!!

NOTHING CAN SAVE YOU FROM ME NOW, PRINCE OF EVIL!

STOP, ACCURSED BROTHER! DO YOU REMEMBER THE NAME OF THIS ISLE... AND THE ONES FOR WHOM IT WAS NAMED?

THE SILENT ONES, WHO LIVE BELOW! THE NATURAL ENEMIES OF THE GODS! ...THE TROLLS!

16.

YOU HAVE BEEN AWAY FROM ASGARD SO LONG THAT YOU MIGHT HAVE FORGOTTEN, *THOR*... HERE WE ARE *ALL* IMMORTALS... WE ARE *ALL* SUPER-POWERFUL!

AND NOTHING THAT LIVES, IN ASGARD OR ON EARTH, CAN BREAK THE GRIP OF A *TROLL!* IT IS FROM *THEM* THAT THE EARTH LEGEND OF THE "OLD MAN OF THE SEA" WAS BORN!

THIS IS THE TRAP I PLANNED FOR YOU, *THOR!* I PROMISED THE *TROLLS* THAT, IF THEY OBEYED ME, I WOULD DELIVER THE *MIGHTIEST* OF THE GODS TO THEM! NOW THEY'LL DRAG YOU BELOW, WHERE YOU SHALL SLAVE IN THEIR MINES FOREVER!

NOT *YET*, EVIL ONE! NOT WHILE I HAVE ONE HAND FREE AND CAN STILL POUND MY ENCHANTED MALLET ON THE GROUND!

FOR, REMEMBER... I AM STILL GOD OF THE THUNDER, AND THE BLAZING LIGHTNING!

LIGHTNING SO *BRIGHT* THAT THE SENSITIVE EYES OF A *TROLL*, USED TO DWELLING IN SEMI-DARK-NESS, CANNOT *BEAR* IT!

AND NOW THAT HE HAS FLED BACK TO THE STYGIAN DEPTHS FROM WHENCE HE CAME, IT IS TIME FOR *YOU* TO TASTE THE AWESOME VENGEANCE OF *THOR!*

STOP, THUNDER GOD! YOU HAVE NOT DEFEATED *LOKI* YET!

I-I SWUNG MY HAMMER RIGHT *THROUGH* YOU!

NOT THROUGH *ME*, FOOL! THROUGH A MENTAL *IMAGE* OF ME! REMEMBER, *LOKI* CAN MATCH YOU, TRICK FOR TRICK, AND *THEN* SOME!

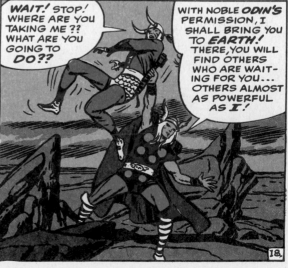

MEANWHILE, BACK ON EARTH, THE INCREDIBLE *HULK* EXECUTES ANOTHER OF HIS AWESOME LEAPS IN HIS EFFORT TO ESCAPE FROM *IRON MAN!*

CAPTAIN! DO *YOU* SEE WHAT *I* SEE?

IT'S THE *HULK*, MAKING ONE OF HIS PRODIGIOUS LEAPS!

SECONDS LATER, AN URGENT RADIO MESSAGE IS HEARD ABOARD THE SAME JETLINER...

ATTENTION, FLIGHT 738! THIS IS *IRON MAN!* HAVE YOU SEEN THE *HULK?* REPEAT -- *HAVE YOU SEEN THE HULK?!*

SUFFERIN' CATS!!

HE..HE JUST WHIZZED PAST US! LOOKED LIKE HE WAS HEADIN' TOWARD DETROIT!

MUCH OBLIGED, CAPTAIN!

EVEN THOUGH I *SEE* IT...I DON'T BELIEVE IT!

FINALLY, ON THE GROUND AGAIN, INSIDE A HUGE AUTO FACTORY...

IRON MAN'S STILL AFTER ME! CAN'T LOSE HIM!

ATTENTION! CLEAR OUT, *ALL* OF YOU! THE *HULK* MUST BE STOPPED! TAKE COVER!

IT'S *IRON MAN!* BOY! HE DOESN'T HAVETA TELL ME *TWICE!*

YOU'RE WASTIN' YOUR TIME, *IRON MAN!* THESE PUNY THINGS CAN'T HURT THE *HULK!*

BUT NOW I'M SICK OF RUNNING! NOW IT'S *MY* TURN TO ATTACK!

HELP! SOMEBODY STOP 'IM! HE'S GONNA TEAR THIS PLACE *APART!!*

COME CLOSER, IRON MAN! CLOSER!! AHHH... NOW!!

WHUMP!

OOOOF!!

STAGGERED BY THE IMPACT, WHICH WOULD HAVE STOPPED ANYTHING OF MERE FLESH, IRON MAN SOON REGAINS HIS BALANCE AND THEN...

ALL RIGHT, HULK! I TRIED TO REASON WITH YOU, BUT NOW...

...I'LL PLAY IT YOUR WAY! FIRST, I'LL RESHAPE THIS SHAFT INTO A STEEL GRAPPLE!

...AND THEN, I'LL USE THE POWERS OF MY TRANSISTORS TO HURL IT WITH PINPOINT ACCURACY!

HAH! BULL'S EYE!

YOU THINK THIS CAN TRAP ME!?

I NEVER EXPECTED THAT! HE PUSHED HIMSELF BACK, RIGHT THROUGH THE WALL!

GOT TO GET OUT! NEED ROOM TO MOVE! ROOM TO FIGHT!

20.

One thing you've gotta admit about The Avengers—they don't kid around!

When they finish off an epic series, they do it in a biiiiig way! Like the story that follows...the title'll give you a clue—it's "Death of a Galaxy!"

You see, a lot has happened since those early days when the world's most powerful superhero team was formed. The Avengers kept fighting foes that were more and more powerful, foes that could conquer entire planets, even galaxies!

Of course, what else wouldja expect? You can't have the mighty Avengers tackling litterbugs or a pickpocket—unless he was dumb enough to pick one of their own pockets!

Anyway, you're about to be bedazzled by the conclusion of "Operation: Galactic Storm" in which two of the most powerful empires in the galaxy (the Shi'ar and the Kree) wage a deadly interstellar war— with Earth caught in the middle! Now *that's* a case for the Avengers!

And if you don't think we knocked ourselves out to find the most exciting tale of all, look at what lies ahead—the Shi'ar have just unleashed the deadliest bomb in history against the Kree—an explosion that poses a terrible moral problem for our heroes, and actually turns Avenger against Avenger!

Look, we try our best to satisfy our readers, but if you're expecting an old-fashioned happy ending, you just may be in for a shock. Can't tell you any more or it won't be a surprise.

Enjoy! We'll meetcha at the next story. . .

THE NEGA-BOMB — AN ANTI-MATTER DEVICE CAPABLE OF SPEWING FORTH DEADLY RADIATION AT TRANS-LIGHT SPEED — WAS BUILT BY THE ALIEN SHI'AR TO END THEIR MONTHS OLD CONFLICT WITH THE KREE. BUT WHEN THE SHI'AR EMPRESS DECIDED NOT TO EMPLOY THE DEVICE, THE KREE'S ANCIENT ENEMIES, THE SKRULLS, STOLE THE BOMB. NOW IT'S BEEN DETONATED AND THE AVENGERS HAVE BEEN CAUGHT IN THE BLAST...!

STAN LEE PRESENTS...

OPERATION: GALACTIC STORM
PART 19

THE AVENGERS

HE IS FULLY ONE AND A HALF MILLION MILES DISTANT WHEN IT EXPLODES...

...AND ALL HOPE WITHIN HIM DIES.

HE STARES IN HORROR AS IT RUSHES RELENTLESSLY TOWARD HIM...

...OBLITERATING EVERYTHING IN ITS PATH.

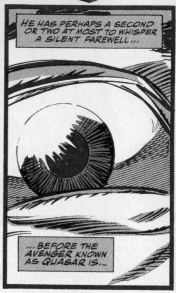

HE HAS PERHAPS A SECOND OR TWO AT MOST TO WHISPER A SILENT FAREWELL...

...BEFORE THE AVENGER KNOWN AS QUASAR IS...

...BLOWN AWAY.

empire's end

THE EPIC CONCLUSION OF THE KREE-SHI'AR WAR BROUGHT TO YOU BY:

BOB HARRAS — WRITER

STEVE EPTING — PENCILER

TOM PALMER — INKER

GINA GOING — COLORIST

BILL OAKLEY
MICHAEL HIGGINS — LETTERERS

RALPH MACCHIO — EDITOR

TOM DEFALCO — EDITOR IN CHIEF

A MOMENT AGO, THIS PROUD STAR CRUISER OF THE IMPERIAL KREE FLEET WAS RETURNING HOME AFTER A THREE YEAR MISSION IN DEEP SPACE...

...IT IS A HOMECOMING THAT IS DESTINED TO NEVER HAPPEN.

< CAPTAIN, WE'RE REGISTERING A MASSIVE ANOMALY ON THE OMNI-WAVE BAND... >

< ...AND SENSORS ARE PICKING UP AN ENERGY FORCE OF ENORMOUS PROPORTIONS EMANATING FROM THE VERY HEART OF THE EMPIRE! >

< NOTIFY HALA AND PUT IT ON THE SCREEN-- QUICKLY! >

< BY THE GREAT PAMA-- WHAT HAS HAPPENED TO THE EMPIRE?! >

ALERT! ALERT! PLASMA WAVE ON INTERSECT VECTOR! COLLISION IMMINENT!

< HELMSMAN, QUICKLY! HARD TO PORT! >

< HARD TO--! >

A MOMENT... THE SPACE BETWEEN ONE HEARTBEAT AND THE NEXT...

...SO SHORT A PERIOD OF TIME...

...BUT FOR THE STAR-FLUNG KREE, CONQUERORS OF A THOUSAND, THOUSAND WORLDS, PROUD MASTERS OF DESTINY, IT IS ALL THE BREADTH OF TIME BETWEEN EXISTENCE...

137

...AND OBLITERATION.

A MOMENT AGO, SACRED HALA, HOMEWORLD OF THE KREE AND CAPITAL OF THEIR VAST EMPIRE, ORBITED ITS SUN PAMA AS IT HAS SINCE CREATION.

HALA— A PLANET BOASTFUL OF ITS HISTORY AND FEARED THROUGHOUT KNOWN SPACE FOR ITS POWER.

BUT THAT WAS BEFORE THE FIRST SHOCK WAVE HIT, RIPPING AWAY THE PLANET'S FAMED DEFENSIVE RINGS LIKE SO MUCH CHAFF IN THE WIND...

...BEFORE THE LORDLY TOWERS OF KREE-LAR, BUILT OVER THE MILLENNIUM TO REMIND THOSE WHO PASSED BENEATH THEIR MASSIVE STRUCTURES OF THE GLORY THAT IS ALL THINGS KREE...

...FELL AMIDST THE ROARING WINDS OF DESTRUCTION.

BEFORE THE KREE LOOKED UP IN HORROR AND CONFUSION AS THEY SAW THEIR WORLD END AROUND THEM...

...CRYING OUT FOR SALVATION FROM UNHEEDING GODS EVEN AS THEIR LIVES ARE RIPPED AWAY.

AND EVEN THOSE WHO KNOW WHERE THIS TERRIBLE RETRIBUTION TRULY CAME FROM...

...CAN ONLY STARE IN SHOCK AT WHAT THE WRATH OF HER PEOPLE HAS FINALLY WROUGHT...

...AS HALA, FAMED HALA FALLS.

BUT THIS FATE WAS NOT MEANT FOR HALA ALONE.

NO, THE BLAST WAVE TRAVELS FAR AND FAST, ENGULFING ALL THE THOUSAND SOLAR SYSTEMS THAT BOWED BEFORE THE EMPIRE. NOTHING IS SPARED THAT CALLED ITSELF KREE.

ON THOSE WORLDS FAR, FAR FROM THE EPICENTER, IT SWEEPS ACROSS THE FACE OF EACH PLANET LIKE THE ANGEL OF DEATH.

SILENTLY, WHOLE POPULACES DIE, NEVER KNOWING THEIR DAY WAS DONE, THEIR TIME FINISHED.

NOT SO OTHER PLANETS NEARER THE CENTER OF THE EMPIRE. THEY DO NOT DIE QUIETLY...

...AS THE SHOCK WAVE RIPS THROUGH THEIR ATMOSPHERE, LEVELING PROUD CITIES AND HUMBLE HOVELS WITH INDISCRIMINATE CONTEMPT...

...THESE WORLDS FAIRLY SCREAM OUT THEIR DEATH CRY.

BUT NOTHING IS ABSOLUTE IN THIS UNIVERSE...

...FOR ON WORLD AFTER WORLD, PITIFUL SUR- VIVORS LOOK UP AT BLAZING SKIES AND WONDER...

...WHAT HAVE THE KREE DONE TO DESERVE THIS?

FAR BEYOND THE BORDER-LANDS, ON THE OUTER FRINGES OF THE GREATER MAGELLANIC CLOUD...

...LIES A RING OF CLOAKED INTER-STELLAR LISTEN-ING POSTS...

...STEALTH CRAFT SENT FROM THE KREE'S GREAT ENEMY, THE SHI'AR IMPERIUM, TO SPY UPON THE EMPIRE -- A TASK THAT IS RAPIDLY BECOMING OBSOLETE.

‹BY SHARRA!›

‹I NEED TACTICAL-- NOW!›

‹DATA FROM OUR LONG RANGE PROBES REPORT *EXTREME* ENERGY FLUCTUATIONS ACROSS THE SPECTRUM, MILORD.

SCANS INDICATE *NEGATIVELY-CHARGED* ENERGY MATRICES APPEARING THROUGHOUT THE KREE TERRI-TORIES.›

‹ RAW GRAVIMETRIC READINGS DETECT *NO* STELLAR OR PLANETARY DISINTEGRATION AT PRESENT.

IN SHORT, MILORD CAPTAIN, ALL IS WITHIN THE PARAMETERS EXPECTED FROM THE DETONATION OF THE NEGA-BOMB.›

‹SO IT IS DONE.›

‹COMMUNICATIONS, OPEN AN INSTA-LINK WITH IMPERIAL CENTER...›

‹...AND REPORT TO THE MAJESTRIX-SHI'AR LILANDRA...›

‹...THE NEWS SHE HAS SO LONG AWAITED...›

‹...THE KREE EMPIRE IS NO MORE.›

THERE IS ONLY A MOURNFUL WIND ON HALA NOW....

...A CONSTANT WIND BLOWING THROUGH THE RUINS, THAT NEARLY DROWNS OUT THE MURMURING OF A WANDERING LOST SOUL....

...THE MADWOMAN CALLED DEATHBIRD.

BUT, NO-- I WALK ALONE AMONG AN EMPIRE OF CORPSES AND YET I STILL LIVE!

IS IT PUNISHMENT, PERHAPS? FOR THIS CRIME IS SHI'AR... AND MY SINS ARE LEGION.

O, AERIE, WE HAVE BROUGHT THE KREE LOW, INDEED...

...BUT NEED WE HAVE KILLED THEM ALL?

O WRETCHED LILANDRA, MY SWEET, GENTLE SISTER... DID YOU IN TRUTH ORDER THIS?

HOW BLOODTHIRSTY YOU'VE BECOME, SISTER. HOW LIKE ME, YOUR HATED RIVAL.

HERE IN THEIR SHATTERED CITADEL, I SHALL BEG FORGIVENESS...

LILANDRA, HOW LIKE YOU I NOW BECOME...

...FOR I SUDDENLY FIND MYSELF FEARING FOR MY SOUL.

BUT YOU FEARED THE NEGA-BOMB. YOU FEARED IT WOULD COST YOU YOUR IMMORTAL SOUL! AND STILL YOU USED IT....!

DID YOU FIND IN YOUR HEART THAT COLD HARD PLACE ALL LEADERS MUST HAVE, SISTER? HOW I WISH I HAD WITNESSED THAT!

THE AVENGER, CAPTAIN AMERICA!

EVEN HERE IN THE KREE IMPERIAL CHAMBER THERE IS DEATH!

YOU SHOULD HAVE STAYED ON EARTH, TERRAN, AND LIVED TO AN OLD AGE.

FOR OUR ANCIENT WAR HAD NOTHING TO DO WITH YOU.

DEEP SPACE...

...WHERE QUASAR BEARS A HEAVY BURDEN...

I FOUND THE QUINJET'S WRECKAGE... NOT THAT THERE WAS MUCH LEFT...

...THE IMPACT MUST HAVE BEEN INCREDIBLE.

THIS SHOULDN'T HAVE HAPPENED! IT WASN'T SUPPOSED TO BE LIKE THIS! WE WERE GOING TO STOP THE WAR... NOT DIE IN IT!

OH, MAN -- HOW AM I GOING TO TELL JARVIS--?

AND LUNA! SHE'S JUST A BABY. TO LOSE HER MOTHER NOW--

HEY--

HEY--

HEY!

WHA--?!

WENDELL!

MAN, ARE YOU A SIGHT FOR SORE EYES, BUDDY!

THOR-- LEGGO! LET GO!

HEY--SORRY.

YOU DON'T UNDERSTAND, THOR.

THE OTHERS-- THE AVENGERS WHO WENT TO HALA-- THEY WERE CAUGHT IN THE NEGABOMB EXPLOSION--

--THEY WERE KILLED, THOR!

DON'T YOU SEE? THEY'RE DEAD! DEAD!

143

NO.

ALL OF THEM? I CAN'T BELIEVE IT.

BELIEVE IT.

I-I COULDN'T FIND CAP.

HE MUST STILL BE OUT THERE... ALONE.

BUT... YOU GUYS PULLED THROUGH OKAY?

WE'RE BATTERED AND BRUISED, QUASAR, BUT WE RODE OUT THE BLAST WAVE WITH MINIMAL DAMAGE.

CAPTAIN MARVEL!

THEN AT LEAST THE SHI'AR ENVOY MADE IT.

I ONLY WISH THAT WERE TRUE, WENDELL.

BUT WONDER MAN AND THE VISION WERE TRAPPED ON THE NEGA-BOMB WHEN IT DETONATED...

...WE WERE ON OUR WAY TO THE BLAST'S EPICENTER WHEN WE PICKED UP YOUR ID BEACON. BELIEVE ME, IT WAS LIKE MUSIC TO OUR EARS.

I JUST WISH CAP AND THE OTHERS COULD HAVE BEEN AS LUCKY.

BRING OUR FRIENDS ABOARD, QUASAR.

WE'LL BRING THEM HOME...

144

--THEY'RE ALIVE!

THEY'RE BOTH ALIVE!

THANK HEAVEN! BUT HOW--

--OH, WHO CARES?! THIS IS INCREDIBLE!

YOU KNOW IT, LADY!

FINALLY SOMETHING'S GONE RIGHT TODAY!

VISION... SIMON...

...I COULDN'T DARE HOPE. I JUST THANK GOD YOU'RE BOTH ALL RIGHT!

OUR SURVIVAL HAD MORE TO DO WITH THE DETONATION'S DIRECTIONAL FORCE THAN ANY DIVINE INTERVENTION, WANDA.

THE CONCUSSIVE BLAST RADIATED OUT FROM THE NEGA-BOMB, LEAVING A VACUUM AT ITS CENTER.

WE FOUND OURSELVES IN A SITUATION NOT UNLIKE THAT OF HIROSHIMA'S PEACE BUILDING WHICH SURVIVED INTACT DESPITE BEING AT THE VERY HEART OF THE FIRST ATOMIC BOMB EXPLOSION.

WHOA, VIZH... SOME TIME FOR HISTORY LESSONS, HUH? TAKIN' NOTES, WANDA...?

HEY! WE'RE ALIVE, MAN...OH, MAN... WE MADE IT THROUGH THE LIGHT.

BUT YOU GOT YOUR WISH, BRO... GENOCIDE... SWEET GENOCIDE... BUT MA EARTH'S SAFE.

YES, INDEED... WHO CARES 'BOUT THE KREE, ANYWAY?

THAT ENERGY FLARE...!

VISION, WHAT'S HAPPENED TO SIMON?

HE IS OBVIOUSLY DISORIENTED.

I WOULD HYPOTHESIZE THAT HIS BODY'S IONIC MOLECULAR STRUCTURE IS ATTEMPTING TO ABSORB THE SUBSTANTIAL AMOUNT OF NEGA-RADIATION IT WAS EXPOSED TO.

I SHOULD ADD THAT A MUTAGENETIC RESPONSE TO THIS ASSIMILATION IS STATISTICALLY POSSIBLE.

HEY, I'M STARVING! ANYONE GOT A PASTRAMI SANDWICH?

STARFOX, WHY DON'T YOU COME JOIN THE OTHERS? THERE'S NOTHING YOU CAN DO BACK HERE.

I KNOW, CAPTAIN.

IT'S JUST THAT I CAN'T SHAKE THE FEELING I'M MISSING SOMETHING...

...THAT...

OF COURSE!

SERSI, YOU CLEVER GIRL, YOU! WE ETERNALS PLAYED THIS GAME AS CHILDREN CENTURIES AGO!

IT'S TIME TO RETURN TO THE LAND OF THE *LIVING*, AVENGERS!

SWWMMMMMM

WELCOME BACK, COUSIN. YOU GAVE US QUITE A FRIGHT!

JUST AS WE USED TO GIVE OUR PARENTS, EH, EROS?

...WHEN IT BECAME APPARENT WE COULD NOT OUTRUN THE SHOCK WAVE AND *DEATH* WAS A *CERTAINTY*...

...I USED MY TRANSMUTATION POWER TO PSIONICALLY *CHANGE* THE MOLECULAR STRUCTURE OF OUR BODIES INTO BASIC *INERT* MATTER...

...*GAMBLING* THAT IN *THAT* FORM WE COULD SURVIVE BOTH THE EXPLOSION AND THE EXPOSURE TO SPACE.

THE *DOWN* SIDE, OF COURSE, WAS THAT WE WOULD BE *LEFT* IN THAT STATE DRIFTING THROUGH SPACE FOR *ETERNITY*...

...UNLESS *ANOTHER* ETERNAL HAPPENED TO STUMBLE UPON US, AND *REVERSE* THE PROCESS.

A PART OF YOUR PLAN I *HAPPILY* FULFILLED, SERSI.

BUT, SERSI, WHERE IS CAPTAIN *AMERICA*?

BELIEVE ME, WE WISH WE *KNEW*, WANDA...

...WE WERE *SEPARATED* BACK ON THE PLANET.

WE *WOULDA* KNOWN, KNIGHT...

...IF IRON MAN HERE HADN'T ORDERED US ALL OFF HALA.

AND YOU KNOW IF WE *HAD* SEARCHED FOR HIM, HAWKEYE, WE WOULD HAVE BEEN ON-PLANET WHEN THE BOMB WENT OFF!

IT WAS THE TOUGHEST DECISION OF MY LIFE, AVENGER, BUT IT WAS A *FAR* SIDE BETTER THAN *SUICIDE*!

THEN CAP'S *STILL* ON HALA?!

WE GOTTA GO *GET* HIM!!

QUASAR, *LISTEN* TO ME...

...WE DON'T EVEN *KNOW* IF HALA STILL EXISTS. THE *CHANCES* THAT CAP IS ALIVE ARE *REMOTE* AT BEST.

SO THAT MEANS WE *GIVE UP* ON HIM, SHELLHEAD?

OF COURSE *NOT*!

I JUST WANT TO MAKE THE *REALITY* OF THE SITUATION CLEAR... SO THERE'S NO FALSE HOPE.

BUT AVENGERS ALWAYS TAKE CARE OF THEIR *OWN*...

...CAPTAIN MARVEL, PLOT A COURSE FOR HALA!

HALA.

YOU *WERE A NOBLE* WARRIOR, TERRAN.

A MAN OF SPIRIT AND METTLE WHO DID BATTLE BRAVELY AGAINST THE KREE AND--

BLOOD AND FIRE--! YOU STILL *BREATHE!*

DO THE FATES THEN *RELENT* IN THEIR CRUEL JUDGMENT?

AM I *NOT* TO BE LEFT ALONE TO RULE A DEAD WORLD?

YOU *ARE* FAIR OF FACE AND PLEASING IN *FORM*...

...A FITTING CONSORT, PERHAPS...

...TO ONE WHO WAS ONCE MAJESTRIX-SHI'AR...

HUH?

DEATH-BIRD--!

--WHAT'S GOING ON, LADY?!

WHY ASK SUCH A QUESTION OF ONE WHO HAS BEEN AS MUCH A PAWN IN THIS AFFAIR AS YOU, CAPTAIN AMERICA?

ALL YOU NEED TO KNOW IS THAT THE LONG STAGNATION IS OVER AND THE DESTINY OF THE KREE IS NOW ASSURED!

THE SUPREME INTELLIGENCE?!

LIGHT YEARS AWAY...

...LIES THE ADMINISTRATIVE HUB OF THE GALAXY-SPANNING SHI'AR IMPERIUM...

...THE THRONE-WORLD CALLED CHANDILAR...

...WHERE NEWS HAS ARRIVED THAT WILL FOREVER CHANGE THE COURSE OF HISTORY.

NEWS THAT MUST BE BROUGHT TO HER WHO IS THE HEART AND SOUL OF THIS EMPIRE...

...LILANDRA, MAJESTRIX-SHI'AR!

<YOU SOUGHT AN AUDIENCE, MY EXECUTIVE COUNCIL?

I TRUST THERE IS WORD.>

<..., NOR, I DARESAY, WILL ANY OTHER POWER. THE PRE-EMINENCE OF THE IMPERIUM HAS BEEN ASSURED THROUGHOUT THE GALAXY.>

<INDEED, AND IT IS ONE OF JOY, EMINENCE, FOR NEVER WAS THERE SUCH A DAY IN SHI'AR HISTORY!

OUR RIGHTEOUS CAUSE HAS TRIUMPHED! THE WAR IS OVER. THANKS TO YOUR DOOMSDAY WEAPON, WE HAVE ACHIEVED AN UNPRECEDENTED VICTORY OVER THE KREE, WHO WILL THREATEN US NO MORE...>

<THE FLEET IS BEING MADE READY EVEN NOW...

...FOR THE GLORY OF THIS DAY IS YOURS>

<MAJESTY?>

<VICTORY, NOBLE LORDS, CAN HAVE A BITTER TASTE.>

<LEAVE ME NOW TO REVEL IN IT.>

OF COURSE. I KNEW SUCH A DEADLY DEVICE WAS NEEDED TO PUSH MY PEOPLE THROUGH THE THRESHOLD...

...BUT I ALSO KNEW IT UNWISE TO BE *DIRECTLY* INVOLVED IN THE CREATION OF SUCH A DOOMS-DAY WEAPON...

...FOR MY PEOPLE ARE *ALSO* LIMITED IN THEIR CONCEPTIONS AND WOULD NOT UNDERSTAND THE NEED FOR SUCH *EXTREME* MEASURES.

I FOUND IT *EXPEDIENT*, THEN, TO REACH ACROSS THE STARS AND PLANT THE IDEA FOR THE NEGA-BOMB UNAWARES IN THE CONSCIOUSNESS OF OUR ANCIENT RIVALS, THE SHI'AR.

THEN, BY *INTENSIFYING* LONG-SUPPRESSED SUSPICIONS AND HATREDS THAT LAY DORMANT IN THE MINDS OF THE LEADERS OF OUR INDIVIDUAL EMPIRES, I *ENGINEERED* THE START OF THE WAR AND *INSURED* TODAY'S OUTCOME.

AND YOU *DARED* USE MY PEOPLE!!

YOU *USED* ME!

DEATHBIRD-- IT'S NO USE!

SMASH

THE KREE MAY HAVE *LOST* THIS DAY... AND OUR NAME MAY *FADE* FROM THE *ANNALS* OF HISTORY...

...BUT MINE IS THE *ETERNAL* VISION, AND IN MILLENNIA TO COME, WE SHALL *EVOLVE* INTO THE RACE WE WERE MEANT TO BE... AND ON THAT DAY -- THE UNIVERSE WILL *TREMBLE!*

AND BILLIONS DIED FOR THIS?! YOU *PITIFUL* PATHETIC--

LET IT *GO*, DEATH-BIRD.

LEAVE HIM TO HIS *CONSCIENCE*...

...IF HE HAS ONE.

OUTSIDE...

...THE AVENGERS MAKE THEIR RETURN TO HALA.

VOOSSH

SWEET AGON!

THIS WAS A CITY -- VASTER THAN ANY I'D EVER SEEN!

AND NOW--!

--NOW--

OH, SWEET AGON!

CAPTAIN MARVEL, LIVING LIGHTNING--

--SCOUT AHEAD. SEE IF YOU CAN FIND ANYONE ALIVE.

CRYSTAL, ARE YOU ALL RIGHT?

MAYBE YOU SHOULD GO BACK TO THE SHIP.

IT'S A WOMAN AND HER CHILD, DANE.

JUST A CHILD... LIKE LUNA.

HOW CAN INTELLIGENT BEINGS HATE EACH OTHER ENOUGH TO DO THIS?

HERC, BUD... I DUNNO IF I CAN TAKE ALL THIS...

...MAYBE I'M NOT TOUGH ENOUGH FOR YOU BIG GUNS. MAYBE I OUGHTA JUST BOW OUT OF THE AVENGERS.

NAY, YOURS IS A SOUL NOBLE AND TRUE, FRIEND ERIC...

"...ON THE MORN YOU DOTH GAZE UPON SUCH CARNAGE AND NOT BE SICKENED TO THY VERY SOUL...

"...THAT WILL BE THE DAY YOU SHOULD COME TO ME AND LEAVE OUR STAUNCH FELLOWSHIP."

SHELLHEAD, BACK ON THE QUINJET, I SAID SOME THINGS I DIDN'T MEAN.

I CAN BE A REAL DUNCE SOMETIMES, Y'KNOW?

WE'VE BEEN FRIENDS A LONG TIME, CLINT--

--IF WE CAN'T DISAGREE, WHO CAN?

WANDA, ARE YOU UNWELL?

IT'S JUST SO...

...OVERWHELMING.

I NEED A MINUTE.

TAKE ALL THE TIME YOU NEED, AVENGERS...

...WHY SHOULDN'T YOU?

THE KREE LIE DEFEATED AT YOUR FEET. OUR CIVILIZATION IS DESTROYED.

YOU HAVE YOUR PRECIOUS VICTORY.

ATLAS AND MINERVA-- --ALIVE?!

KREEMAN-- HEAR ME--THIS IS NO VICTORY FOR THE AVENGERS! WE DIDST E'ER SEEK TO PREVENT THIS DISASTER!

AND TO OUR EVERLASTING SORROW, WE FAILED.

WE CAN BUT OFFER OUR SYMPATHY AND ASSISTANCE IN THIS AWFUL AFTERMATH.

DO YOU THINK ME A FOOL, HERCULES?

MY PEOPLE ARE DEAD--

--AND YOU OF ALL PEOPLE OFFER US PITY?!

MURDERERS!!

ATLAS, YOU IDIOT--!

WE'RE TELLING YOU THE *TRUTH!*

WE DIDN'T DO THIS!

C'MON, HAWK...

...LOOKS LIKE THE GOD SQUAD COULD USE A HAND.

YEAH...BUT WHAT ABOUT HIS *PLAYMATE,* MINERVA?

I WOULDN'T WORRY ABOUT *HER,* AVENGER...

...SERSI AND I HAVE MATTERS WELL IN HAND.

OOOBOY... THAT JOKER'S GOT SOME HOOK!

COME ON, ATLAS, GIVE UP! THERE'S NO *POINT* TO FIGHTING ANY MORE, GUY!

THEN *KILL* ME, ASSASSINS...

...FOR WITHOUT MY PEOPLE--I DO NOT WANT TO LIVE--KILL ME!

STOP!!

THERE'S BEEN ENOUGH KILLING TODAY.

SO -- BEHOLD THE EVIDENCE THAT MAKES MOCKERY OF YOUR WORDS...

YOUR LEADER AND DEATHBIRD -- TOGETHER. CAN YOU DENY NOW THAT YOU WERE EVER IN LEAGUE WITH THE SHI'AR?

FOOL!

THERE WAS NO ALLIANCE... SAVE FOR THE UNWITTING ONE WE ALL PARTICIPATED IN AT THE HANDS OF THE SUPREME INTELLIGENCE.

LOOK AROUND YOU AND SEE THE CULMINATION OF YOUR LEADER'S DREAMS.

IT WAS HE WHO DID THIS. HE WHO CREATED EVENTS THAT LED TO THE NEGA-BOMB. HE WHO KILLED THE KREE!

STOP THIS BLASPHEMY, SHI'AR -- OR I SWEAR I WILL RIP THE WORDS OUT OF YOUR MOUTH!

TRY, KREEMAN, AND IT WILL BE THE LAST THING YOU EVER DO.

THAT'S ENOUGH, DEATHBIRD.

THOR, WOULD YOU TAKE CARE OF MISS CHARMING?

TELL HIM, TERRAN... HOW HIS BELOVED LEADER SLAUGHTERED HIS OWN PEOPLE! HOW HE GLOATED IN HIS VICTORY!

TELL HIM!!

I KNOW IT'S HARD TO BELIEVE, ATLAS, BUT SHE'S TELLING THE TRUTH.

THE SUPREME INTELLIGENCE HAD THIS PLANNED FROM THE BEGINNING. THE NEGA-BOMB WAS MEANT TO MUTATE THE KREE, TO JUMPSTART YOUR EVOLUTIONARY DEAD-END.

APPARENTLY, IT WORKED. HE'S UP THERE IN THE CITADEL, BASKING OVER HIS 'TRIUMPH.'

I REJECT THIS! WHO COULD BELIEVE SUCH A TALE?!

TELL HIM, MINERVA.

YOU KNEW ALL ALONG, DIDN'T YOU?

IT STANDS TO REASON. YOU WERE THE ONLY SCIENTIST ON STARFORCE. YOU'VE DEDICATED YOUR LIFT TO 'IMPROVING' THE KREE.

IS THIS WHAT YOU WANTED?

I WANT THE KREE TO SURVIVE, CAPTAIN. IT IS AS SIMPLE AS THAT.

IT IS UNFORTUNATE THAT SUCH A SACRIFICE WAS ASKED OF OUR PEOPLE... BUT, TRUST ME, THE RESULTS WILL BE WELL WORTH IT.

THE OFFSPRING OF THE SURVIVORS SHALL BE THE FIRST OF A NEW BREED... AND YOU WILL FEAR THEM, EARTHMAN. OH, YOU WILL FEAR THEM!

IN PAMA'S NAME, WOMAN-- HOW COULD YOU?!

YOU ARE A TRAITOR TO OUR PEOPLE!

ATLAS... LISTEN--!

OUR DNA HAS BEEN *CHANGED.* THE *POTENTIAL* IS UN-LIMITED NOW, AND *YOU* WERE MEANT TO BE MY *MATE...*

...THINK OF THE WONDROUS GEN-ERATIONS TO COME! THE *GLORY* THAT WILL BE THEIRS! DON'T YOU UNDERSTAND? THE WEAK *HAD* TO *DIE!*

NO, THEY DID NOT.

BUT WE SHALL JOIN THEM.

TEK

CAPTAIN AMERICA, I SUGGEST YOU AND THE AVENGERS SEEK COVER.

I HAVE ENGAGED MY *BATTLE-SUIT'S* SELF-DESTRUCT PRO-GRAM. THE BLAST SHALL BE QUITE... *VIOLENT.*

GOOD LORD, ATLAS-- DON'T DO THIS!

I *MUST,* CAPTAIN. I SEE NOW THAT MY LIFE HAS BEEN A *LIE.* I HAVE SERVED A *MONSTER* WITH *ALL* MY HEART AND SOUL...

...AND IN DOING SO I AM AS *CULPABLE* AS HE FOR WHAT HAS HAPPENED HERE.

I SALUTE YOU, *AVENGERS.* YOU ARE INDEED WORTHY OF *RESPECT.*

I *BEG* YOU... DO WHAT I *CANNOT...* MAKE THE SUPREME INTELLIGENCE PAY FOR HIS CRIME.

DESTROY HIM SO HIS VICTIMS MAY REST IN PEACE.

ATT-LASS!

YOU DON'T *UNDERSTANNND*...

VMMMMMMMMMMMMMMMMMMMMMMMM...

GOOD LORD.

YOU HEARD HIM, FOLKS.

LET'S KILL THAT SCUM.

DANE-- NO! STOP!

WHA--?!

CAP, YOU CAN'T MEAN TO LET THAT MURDERER GO!

DON'T YOU THINK I'M SICKENED BY WHAT'S HAPPENED HERE, IRON MAN?

BUT KILL? IN COLD BLOOD? THE SUPREME INTELLIGENCE IS A SENTIENT BEING... TO KILL HIM IS... UNTHINKABLE.

LET THE KREE SURVIVORS HANDLE THIS. THE WAR IS OVER... THE STARGATES WON'T BE USED AGAIN. EARTH IS SAFE.

THERE'S NOTHING MORE WE CAN DO. DEAR GOD, WE CAN'T BRING BACK THE DEAD.

CAPTAIN, I AM NOT PERSUADED THE SUPREME INTELLIGENCE MEETS THE CRITERIA FOR ARTIFICIAL LIFE WHICH SEEMS TO BE DISTURBING YOU. THUS, THE WORD "KILL" WOULD BE INAPPROPRIATE IN THIS SITUATION.

THE INTELLIGENCE CAN ALSO BE DEFINED AS NOTHING MORE THAN AN EXTREMELY COMPLEX COMPUTER. SEEN IN THIS LIGHT, THERE CAN BE NO MORAL COMPUNCTION IN SHUTTING IT DOWN.

THE VISION SPEAKS THE TRUTH, AVENGERS!

THIS IS AN EVIL THAT MUST BE STOPPED! NO PLAINER COURSE HAS E'ER STOOD BEFORE US!

IT IS MONSTROUS THAT WE DOTH DEBATE WHEN THE BODIES OF HIS VICTIMS LIE AROUND US! BILLIONS HAVE DIED THIS DAY!

BUT, HERCULES... IF HE IS A LIVING THING...

...WE DON'T HAVE THE RIGHT TO SIMPLY... KILL.

AND IF WE DON'T, CRYSTAL...?

WHAT IF NEXT TIME, HIS PLANS INCLUDE DOING THIS TO EARTH? WHAT ABOUT HUMANITY'S RIGHTS, THEN?

HERCULES IS RIGHT! LOOK AROUND YOU, MAN!

BY ZURAS, THIS WAS GENOCIDE! IS THERE ICE IN YOUR VEINS?!

SERSI... BELIEVE ME, MY GUT WANTS HIM TO PAY AS MUCH AS YOU.

BUT WE CANNOT KILL. WE ARE NOT JUDGE, JURY AND EXECUTIONER. IT IS AS SIMPLE AS THAT.

IT IS AS SIMPLE AS VENGEANCE, CAPTAIN! A MATTER OF RIGHT OVER WRONG!

OKAY, THAT'S ENOUGH.

IRON MAN?!

FSHAMM

I'M THE ONLY ORIGINAL AVENGER PRESENT... AND I'M PULLING RANK, CAP.

I DON'T AGREE WITH YOU. THE SUPREME INTELLIGENCE IS A MACHINE... A SOULLESS PIECE OF HARDWARE...

...THAT WE WILL DESTROY SO THAT NOTHING LIKE THIS WILL EVER HAPPEN AGAIN.

WHO'S WITH ME?

I'M SORRY, CAP.

MAYBE WE CAN'T BRING THE DEAD BACK... BUT WE CAN AT LEAST AVENGE 'EM.

HECK... IT'S OUR NAME!

WELL SAID, KNIGHT. WELL SAID!

I UNDERSTAND -- THEN -- THAT YOU OTHERS AGREE WITH CAP?

YOU UNDERSTAND CORRECTLY, IRON MAN.

MANOMAN, SHELLHEAD... DON'T DO THIS!

WE CANNOT JOIN IN A KILLING EXPEDITION... NO MATTER WHAT THE PROVOCATION.

YEAH. WE'RE THE AVENGERS...

...WE DON'T DO THINGS LIKE THIS!

WHERE, THEN, IS YOUR *PRIDE*, TERRAN?

NO, DEATHBIRD, IT'S ABOUT *JUSTICE*.

YOU, NO LESS THAN I, WERE *USED* IN THIS AFFAIR. THIS IS ABOUT *REVENGE!*

LET'S GO, PEOPLE.

WE HAVE A *JOB* TO DO.

THOR -- LISTEN TO ME, BUD! YOU'RE GETTING INTO *VERY* MUDDY WATERS HERE!

CAP'S RIGHT-- THE INTELLIGENCE IS A *LIVING THING!*

AND IT'S STRICTLY AN AVENGERS AFFAIR. KINDLY BUT OUT.

SIMON, WE ALL MADE A VOW *NEVER* TO KILL.

IF YOU ARE *WRONG* ABOUT THIS, CAN YOU DEAL WITH THE CONSEQUENCES?

WE'RE NOT WRONG, WANDA.

I WISH YOU COULD *SEE* THAT.

YOU ALWAYS THINK CAP'S RIGHT, WENDELL. THAT'S YOUR PROBLEM.

ONE DAY YOU'RE GONNA HAVE TO LEARN TO THINK FOR YOURSELF!

CAPTAIN, I HONOR THEE AS OUR LEADER -- BUT TODAY, THOU ART MOST GRIEVIOUSLY *MISGUIDED*.

TO LET THIS MENACE LIVE *DIS-HONORS* US ALL... AND BRINGS SHAME TO THE NAME AVENGER.

I SEE NOW THAT AT LEAST *SOME* OF YOU KNOW WHAT IT MEANS TO BE A WARRIOR.

SHUT UP, DEATHBIRD!

CAP, DO YOU WANT ME TO *STOP* THEM?

NO.

LET THEM GO.

THE CITADEL.

AH--THE *RENEGADE* AVENGERS. YOU WERE *EXPECTED*.

I MONITORED YOUR *SPIRITED* DEBATE, TERRANS, EVEN AS I NOW SENSE YOUR *DOUBTS*.

YOU PRESENT A FACE OF MORAL *CERTITUDE*, BUT YOU DON'T *REALLY* KNOW, DO YOU? AM I A CONSTRUCT --OR AM I *ALIVE?* YOU *FEAR* THE ANSWER!

YOU'RE *DREAMING*, INTELLIGENCE! WE'RE NOT AFRAID--

--JUST *DETERMINED* TO END YOUR MADNESS *NOW!*

FSSSMMM

I DON'T THINK SO, LITTLE MAN--

--I DON'T THINK SO AT *ALL!*

WHA--?! WHAT'S *HAPPENING?!*

I AM *PROTECTING* MYSELF, AVENGERS, AS ANY LIFE FORM WOULD WHEN UNDER ATTACK.

MY STARFORCE MAY BE OFF-PLANET, BUT DID YOU THINK I WOULD LEAVE MYSELF *TOTALLY* UNDEFENDED?

FROM YOUR MEMORIES I HAVE FOUND THE SEEDS OF YOUR *DEFEAT.*

THAT'S *THOR!* THE *REAL* THOR!

WHAT'S HAPPENED TO HIM?!

CALM DOWN, AVENGER. IT'S NOT HIM

THEY'RE ONLY IMAGES *PLUCKED* FROM OUR MINDS TO CONFUSE US.

THEY ARE *MORE* THAN MERE IMAGES. I HAVE GIVEN THEM FORM AND SUBSTANCE TO *DE-STROY* YOU.

YEAH... BUT DID YOU HAVE TO GO AND PICK MY BROTHER, *ERIC?*

THE *GRIM REAPER,* EH?

DON'T WORRY, SIMON.

ULTRON HAS ALSO BEEN DEFEATED.

IRON MAN, I SHARE YOUR DUBIOUS VIEW OF THIS CHALLENGE. VICTORY HAS BEEN TOO EASILY OBTAINED. THE SUPREME INTELLIGENCE IS UNQUESTIONABLY CAPABLE OF DEFENDING ITSELF MUCH MORE EFFECTIVELY.

THOU DOST THINK *TOO* MUCH, VISION.

THE FOUL MURDERER STANDS BEFORE US. LET US NOT QUESTION PROVIDENCE.

THE QUESTION IS WHY IT HAS CHOSEN NOT TO.

GOTTA AGREE WITH HERK, VIZH.

MAYBE HE WAS *DAMAGED* IN THE EXPLOSION. IT DOESN'T MATTER--

--WE HAVE OUR CHANCE AND WE'RE GONNA *TAKE* IT!

POUR IT *ON*, AVENGERS--

GIVE IT EVERYTHING YOU'VE GOT!

WE *DID* IT. WE *SHATTERED* THE SCREEN!

SMASH

YES, BUT WHAT LIES *BEYOND?*

THE VERY HEART OF THE SUPREME INTELLIGENCE, SERSI. APPARENTLY, WE HAVE FOUND HIS LIFE SUPPORT SYSTEM.

FASCINATING.

THE STRUCTURE SEEMS TO BE AN AMALGAMATION OF ORGANIC TISSUE AND CYBERNETIC MATERIAL.

THE TECHNOLOGY THAT DESIGNED SUCH A CONSTRUCT IS MOST IMPRESSIVE. IT IS RE-GRETTABLE THE KREE CULTURE DID NOT PURSUE A LESS AGRESSIVE PATH.

DID HE SAY ORGANIC-- --AS IN... LIVING?!

WHAT DOES IT MATTER?

IT IS A MATTER OF SEMANTICS.

WE CAME HERE FOR A PURPOSE, THOR--

-- NOW IS NOT THE TIME FOR DOUBTS!

THESE TENTACLES SEEM TO BE SOME SORT OF LAST DEFENSE.

MY SWORD'S HAVING TROUBLE CUTTING THROUGH!

C'MON, THOR, YOU *HEARD* DANE-- --WE COULD USE YOUR *HELP!*

I...I'M NOT SURE... SIMON, I THINK THE INTELLIGENCE IS REALLY *ALIVE*...

...AND I *CAN'T* KILL. I *CAN'T!*

SORRY.

SKREE

THERE YOU GO, KNIGHT...

...THAT TAKES CARE OF THE LAST TENTACLE.

MUCH OBLIGED, SHELLHEAD.

IT'S *DEFENSELESS* NOW...

I JUST HOPE WE'RE RIGHT.

DANE, IF YOU HAVE A SINGLE *DOUBT*...

...THEN STOP!

THERE CAN BE NO ABSOLUTE CERTAINTY AT THIS POINT.

JUST *DO IT!*

REMEMBER WHAT HE *DID!*

HOW *COULD* I FORGET?

SHUNNTT

AIEEEEE!

A PLUNGED SWORD...

...THE AWESOME UNLEASHING OF A VAST, UNTAPPED POWER THAT WAS THE SUPREME INTELLIGENCE...

...THE COLLAPSE OF THE KREE CITADEL.

WHAT THE HECK--?!

FZAMM

SOME SORT OF CONCENTRATED ENERGY BEAM--!

AGAIN IT TAKES BUT THE SPACE OF A HEARTBEAT.

BUT IT IS THE SCREAM...

...THE CRY OF AGONY THAT ECHOES ACROSS THE FALLEN CITY...

...THAT WILL HAUNT THE AVENGERS FOR A LIFETIME.

I SUGGEST WE MAKE HASTE, GENTLEMEN.

YOU DON'T HAVE TO TELL US TWICE, SERSI.

IN THE CHAOS, NO ONE LOOKS UP TO SEE A TINY POINT OF LIGHT RISE UP FROM THE TOWER'S RUINS...

...AND RACE INTO THE DARKLING SKY...

169

MUCH REMAINS TO BE DONE. MUCH PAIN TO BE REDRESSED...

...BUT NONE OF IT IS ANY LONGER YOUR CONCERN, AVENGERS.

YOU HAVE MY WORD THAT THE STARGATE NEAR YOUR SUN WILL NEVER BE USED AGAIN. YOUR WORLD... HOME OF MY HEART... IS ONCE AGAIN SAFE.

WE LIVE IN A UNIVERSE THAT HAS BEEN IRREVOCABLY CHANGED. SUCH CHANGE ALWAYS CARRIES A PRICE.

THE SHI'AR MUST FACE THE CONSEQUENCES OF OUR ACTIONS. BUT WE FACE THEM ALONE.

RETURN TO EARTH AND LEAVE US TO OUR DESTINY.

WE WISH YOU LUCK, LILANDRA. YOU'VE ASSUMED AN AWESOME RESPONSIBILITY. TODAY YOU'VE BECOME ONE OF THE MOST POWERFUL BEINGS IN THE UNIVERSE.

A DAY IN WHICH WE WITNESSED THE EXPRESSION OF AUTHORITY SO ABSOLUTE THAT THE SANCTITY OF LIFE MEANT NOTHING BEFORE THE DESTINY OF EMPIRES AND THE CAUSE OF SELF-RIGHTEOUSNESS.

IT'S A STORY AS OLD AND SAD AS TIME. AND ONE THAT MUST END NOW BEFORE THERE ARE MORE NEGA-BOMBS, MORE DEAD.

YOU HAVE A GREAT OPPORTUNITY TO DO THAT...

...TO BE POWERFUL ENOUGH TO CHERISH LIFE...

...NOT DESTROY IT.

BUT YOU WERE RIGHT ON ONE POINT, MAJESTRIX...

...THINGS WILL *NEVER* BE THE SAME.

EPILOGUE

< SCANNERS ARE PICKING UP THE CAPSULE AT THE *EXACT* COORDINATES WE WERE SUPPLIED WITH...>

< WE'VE LOCKED ONTO IT WITH OUR TRACTOR BEAM, BRINGING IT IN.>

<INITIATING TRANSFERAL TO OUR COMPUTER CORE.>

< BY THE *EVERCHANGING!* I'VE *NEVER* SEEN SUCH COMPLEX DATA FLOW!>

< WHAT DID YOU *EXPECT,* FOOL? IT *IS* THE KNOWLEDGE OF A THOUSAND MILLENNIA.>

NOW DO AS WE WERE INSTRUCTED...PUT *HIM* ON THE SCREEN.

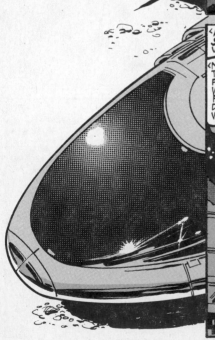

<AH! I SEE THAT I *SURVIVED* AND YOU WERE PUNCTUAL...>

<NOW TAKE ME TO THE *APPOINTED* PLACE WHERE I WILL *AWAIT* THE FRUITS OF THIS DAY. MY PLAN WENT *PERFECTLY...*>

"<...AND I CAN AFFORD TO BE *PATIENT.*>"

END

PART FOUR

AND A BLIND MAN SHALL LEAD THEM

ONE of the things I enjoy the most is lecturing at various college campuses. I try to leave myself at least two days a month in which to dispense my own brand of Marvel madness to keepers of the faith throughout the hallowed halls of academia. When I look at an ever-swelling sea of youthful faces, freshly scrubbed and flushed with the feverish flame of ebullient enthusiasm; when I see the heroic hordes of Marveldom Assembled, bright-eyed and bushytailed, 'tis then I know the cultural bastions of Western Man still stand secure.

But, even as I pen these weighty words, I sense a certain disquietude stirring within your breast. You who treasure the time-honored beginnings of magniloquent Marvel must not be sidetracked by my own mellow musings. Ah yes, I can almost hear you ponder, fondly though firmly, "Hey, what's all this stuff gotta do with the origins of Marvel Comics?" A fair question, fairly stated. I can do no less than to forthrightly reply.

While sagaciously speaking at the various seats of learning which I visit during my tumultuous tours, there is one particular question inevitably hurled at me, namely, "Which is your favorite Marvel Superhero?" (Now do you see how deftly we begin to tie it all together?) Although I love each of our costumed cavorters with the same indelible intensity, even as a father loves his children equally—churlish though some may be—still there is one shining star in the Marvel galaxy whose origin turns me on perhaps a bit more than some of the others. There is one particular character whose creation was somewhat more of a challenge, somewhat more difficult to work out, and somewhat more satisfying to savor when it was finally completed. And now, if you'll forgive me for so circuitous an introduction, we'll hasten to reach the nitty gritty.

One of the things that keeps a fella young in the comicbook business (and might also be the same thing that quickly ages him—but we'll explore that ponderous paradox at some later date) is the necessity to be continually creating new characters and new story concepts. No matter how great, how popular, how successful an existing line of titles may be, the public is ever insatiable in its demand for newer and more varied storylines. And since the primary goal of Marvel Comics is to please the public, it's necessary for us to constantly introduce new and unique heroes with new and unique powers, traits, and attributes. Which brings us to the beginning of 1964, when I was pacing my office one fateful day, seeking the most elusive prey of all—a new idea for a different type of superhero.

Up till now all of our heroes were characters with great powers and some sort of compensatory weaknesses. But always the power was the big thing. In an effort to break the pattern, to alter the formula by coming up with something in a totally new vein, I was trying to think of a hero who would start out with a disability—a hero whose weakness would actually be more colorful, more unusual than his power itself. Not the easiest thing to come up with, perhaps, but I was in there trying.

And then it hit me. I remembered some books I had read years ago, mystery stories about a blind detective named Duncan Maclain. If a man without sight could be a successful detective, think what a triumph it would be to make a blind man a comicbook superhero. The minute I thought about it I loved it. If we could really pull it off, it would give us possibly the most unique action character of all. But I knew there was one tremendous pitfall—how would we make such a character believable? Even though our comics are rooted in the worlds of fantasy and imagination, they still must have a semblance of believability; they still must seem credible, no matter how far-out the basic concept may be. But how were we to make a reader believe that a man without sight could actually perform the hazardous feats of heroism that would be required? This was the problem I was faced with—the problem that had to be solved.

Maybe I'm a glutton for punishment. Maybe too many of our other stories had come to me too easily. Whatever the reason, I find it much more fun when a potential feature has a Gordian knot which must be untied before the plot will work. I'm a fiend for any and all sorts of puzzles, and this particular problem was like settling down with a tough, juicy crossword puzzle that had to be solved.

It didn't happen overnight, but after a while the pieces began to fall slowly into place. It's common knowledge that when a person loses his sight, his other senses usually become somewhat keener as he grows more dependent upon them. Well, I would simply take that premise and expand upon it. But I needed a catalyst—something on which to base our hero's increased sensory powers. And, as we've done so many times in the past, I decided to use an atomic accident, although in a slightly different way. No need to go into detail now; you'll read all about it as soon as I run out of introduction.

Unlike virtually all of our other superheroes, this one, I decided, would forgo the use of super strength completely. The uniqueness of our new character would lie in the fact that his senses of hearing, smell, touch, and taste would be many, many times keener than those of a sighted person. Also, I'd find some excuse to make him a splendidly athletic specimen, to give him a colorful costume, and to create for him some sort of unusual weapon which would be both simple and imaginative. How well we succeeded will be for you to judge—all I can do is feed you the facts, courageously, without fear or favor.

Finding a title was relatively easy in this case. It seemed to me that any man who would become a costumed crime-fighter despite the fact that he had lost his eyesight could certainly be called a daredevil—if not a completely certifiable nut. I liked the name "Daredevil"; it had a certain swashbuckling sound to it. You know, it's a funny thing—as soon as you have a title to work with, everything seems to become easier. It's as though knowing your character's name suddenly unlocks a lot of doors and allows you to invent various aspects of his character and his private life—as though knowing his name actually illuminates him for you. All the details began to hit me fast and furiously, until all that remained was finding the proper artist to bring the whole thing to life. Which brings us to another story.

Among the truly great creators in the annals of comics, the name of Bill Everett must surely hold an honored place high on the list. Big Bill had been the man who created the unforgettable Prince Namor, The Sub-Mariner, one of Marvel's all-time favorite hero/ villains. In fact, along with the early Human Torch, the original Sub-Mariner was featured in the first comicbook we ever published, *Marvel Mystery Comics,* way back in November 1939.

However, since this portion of our captivating chronicle isn't actually concerned with The Sub-Mariner, we'll hopscotch the calendar and leap ahead three decades to 1964 when Bill and I were discussing Daredevil over a couple of cups of coffee. During the past few years, Bill had only been working occasionally in comics and I had been trying for months to lure him back to Marvel as a full-timer. However, he never seemed to find just the right strip that he really could sink his teeth into. But, when I mentioned the general idea of Daredevil, something instantly jelled. The old-time excitement came back into his eyes and he pounded the table, saying "Hey! That's the one I wanna do!"

So happy was I that we'd finally won him back to the fold that I didn't even mention anything about his spilling half a cup of coffee on my freshly scrubbed bluejeans. I gently shoved the bill from my side of the table to his and headed for the door. "See you in the Bullpen!" I shouted, and another merely magnificent Marvel masterwork was under way!

As the days went by and Daredevil started to come to life under the brilliantly stylistic pencil and pen of Bill Everett, I was happy as a lark. One of the truly great talents in our field was back on the Marvel roster once again, and I knew that Daredevil would soon be taking his place alongside Spider-Man, Iron Man, Thor, and all the rest of our best-selling collection of costumed celebrities. I knew that Bill's offbeat and totally different genre of illustration would provide a welcome change-of-pace from our usual superhero style of art. So I predicted. And so it came to pass. So be it.

Oh, one last note before I turn you loose. Of all the many Marvel "repertory groups," perhaps none has changed more often or more steadily than Daredevil and his little supporting cast. Over the years they've added characters and subtracted characters, changed costumes, altered relationships, and generally made it totally impossible for anyone to keep track of what's going on if more than one issue should ever be missed. The Daredevil of 1964 is quite a bit different from the swingin' DD of today, but I think you'll agree, as you proudly peruse the pages to come, that Bill's valorous version was possibly one of the greatest introductory issues of all.

THE ORIGIN OF DAREDEVIL

REMEMBER THIS COVER? IF YOU ARE ONE OF THE FORTUNATE FEW WHO BOUGHT THIS FIRST COPY-- YOU PROBABLY WOULDN'T PART WITH IT FOR ANYTHING!

NOW WE CONGRATULATE YOU FOR HAVING BOUGHT ANOTHER PRIZED FIRST-EDITION! THIS MAGAZINE IS CERTAIN TO BE ONE OF YOUR MOST VALUED COMIC MAG POSSESSIONS IN THE MONTHS TO COME!

WRITTEN BY....... STAN LEE
ILLUSTRATED BY... BILL EVERETT
LETTERED BY...... SAM ROSEN

YOU ARE LOOKING AT THE ENTRANCE TO FOGWELL'S GYM ON NEW YORK'S LOWER WEST SIDE! IT IS HERE THAT OUR STORY BEGINS... A STORY DIFFERENT FROM ANY YOU HAVE EVER READ BEFORE!

IN A DINGY ROOM ABOVE THE GYM, FOUR MEN PLAY A GAME OF POKER, LITTLE DREAMING OF THE SHOCK WHICH AWAITS THEM!

COME ON, PORKY! WE HAVEN'T GOT ALL DAY! *THE FIXER* MAY BE HERE SOON!

KEEP YOUR SHIRT ON, SAM! I DON'T RUSH FOR *ANYONE!*

WHO DO YOU THINK YOU'RE KIDDIN'? YOU KNOW WHEN THE *FIXER* SNAPS HIS FINGERS, WE *ALL* HOP, IF WE WANNA STAY HEALTHY!

SAM'S RIGHT! ANYHOW, I'M BUSHED! LET'S KNOCK OFF FOR A WHILE UNTIL... HEY! WHAT'S THAT NOISE?

CREAK!

FOR THE LUVVA PETE! WHAT DO YA CALL *THAT?!!*

YOU'RE IN THE WRONG PLACE, BUSTER! WE DON'T USE COSTUMED *WRESTLERS* HERE!

I'VE SEEN NUTTY GETUPS, BUT *THAT* ONE TAKES THE CAKE!

BUT LOOK AT HIS *BUILD!* HANG AROUND, FELLA... MAYBE THE *FIXER* CAN USE YOU!

I INTEND TO DO JUST *THAT!* WHEN I'M THROUGH WITH THE *FIXER,* HE'LL NEVER BE ABLE TO USE ANYONE EVER AGAIN!

HEY, THAT GUY'S HERE LOOKIN' FOR *TROUBLE!* THE FIXER WON'T *LIKE* THAT!!

OKAY, MISTER... WE'VE *HAD* IT! NOW WHO *ARE* YOU, AND WHAT DO YOU *WANT*?

IT AIN'T *POSSIBLE!* NOBODY CAN FIGHT LIKE THAT! HE MUST DO IT WITH *MIRRORS!!*

NOW THAT PLAY TIME'S OVER, I'LL HANG AROUND UNTIL I FIND THE *FIXER!* AS FOR WHO I *AM*, YOU CAN JUST CALL ME... *DAREDEVIL!!*

"*DAREDEVIL*"! A BRAND NEW NAME IN THE WORLD OF SUPER HEROES! BUT ONE WHICH IS DESTINED TO REACH THE VERY HEIGHTS OF GLORY! FOR *DAREDEVIL* HAS A *SPECIAL* TYPE OF POWER...SUCH AS NO ADVENTURER HAS EVER HAD BEFORE! TO LEARN WHAT IT IS, LET US GO BACK A FEW YEARS...BACK TO THE *ORIGIN* OF THE MAN CALLED

DAREDEVIL!

THE YEAR IS 1950, AS THE PRIZEFIGHTER KNOWN AS *BATTLING MURDOCK* TALKS TO HIS EIGHT-YEAR OLD SON MATTHEW...

BUT I DON'T *WANT* TO STUDY NOW, DAD! WHY CAN'T I GO OUT AND PLAY BALL WITH THE KIDS? I CAN STUDY LATER ON!

NO, MATT! YOU'LL DO IT *NOW!* YOU'LL STUDY EVERY CHANCE YOU GET, HEAR?

I PROMISED YOUR MOTHER, BEFORE SHE DIED, THAT I WOULDN'T LET YOU GROW UP TO BE AN UNEDUCATED PUG LIKE ME! *YOU'RE* GOING TO AMOUNT TO SOMETHING, MATT!

BUT I *WANT* TO BE LIKE YOU, DAD! I'M *PROUD* OF YOU! YOU'RE THE GREATEST...

DON'T SAY IT, BOY! I'M PAST MY PRIME! I'VE NO FUTURE...NOTHING I CAN DO BUT BECOME A PUNCHING BAG FOR YOUNGER MEN!

BUT I WON'T LET THAT HAPPEN TO *YOU!* YOU'RE GONNA *STUDY*... BECOME A LAWYER, OR A DOCTOR ...YOU'LL *BE* SOMEBODY...THE SOMEBODY THAT I CAN NEVER BE!

NOW GO BACK TO YOUR ROOM, SON... AND GET BUSY WITH YOUR BOOKS!

OKAY, DAD!

5

As the years roll by, Matt Murdock does his best to live up to his father's dream!! He becomes top student in his class, forsaking all sports, all athletic activities, although his heart aches for the thrills of the baseball diamond and the gridiron!

IF ONLY DAD WOULD LET ME TRY OUT FOR THE TEAM! I'D BE AS GOOD AS ANY OF THEM... I JUST KNOW I WOULD!

BUT I CAN'T GO AGAINST HIS WISHES! I CAN'T DEFY DAD, AFTER ALL HE'S DONE FOR ME... AFTER ALL HIS SACRIFICES!... I'VE GOT TO BE THE SON HE WANTS ME TO BE!

And so, young Matt Murdock goes his lonely way, spending every minute he can spare with his books, never sharing in the games of the other teen-agers!

THE KIDS ARE INDIAN RASSLING! IF ONLY I COULD GO DOWN AND JOIN THEM!

No one can be as cruel as an unthinking youth! It is only a matter of time before the neighborhood kids make up a nickname for Matt... a name he will long remember

WELL, WELL! IF IT AIN'T OL' DAREDEVIL HIMSELF!

HI, DAREDEVIL! BE SURE YOU DON'T TIRE YOURSELF OUT TURNING ALL THOSE HEAVY PAGES IN YOUR SCHOOL BOOKS!

THEY'RE LAUGHING AT ME! THEY THINK I'M A SISSY!

Then, when he reaches his room...

SOMEDAY I'LL SHOW THEM! I'LL MAKE THEM EAT THOSE WORDS!

I'M AS STRONG AS ANY OF THEM... AS RUGGED AS ANY OF THEM! AND I'LL PROVE IT! SOMEDAY I'LL PROVE IT!!

His anger boiling within him, the resentful youth strikes out at his dad's punching bag, with the pent-up fury of a thunderclap...

THE DAY WILL COME WHEN NO ONE WILL EVER LAUGH AT ME AGAIN! WHEN... HEY! I...I KNOCKED THE BAG CLEAN OFF!

...HEN, AFTER REPAIRING THE CLASP...

WHAT A **NUMBSKULL** I AM! WHY DON'T I DO THIS **EVERY DAY**!? JUST TO KEEP IN SHAPE!

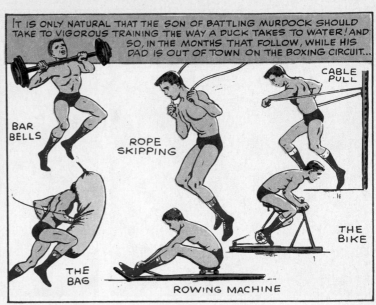

IT IS ONLY NATURAL THAT THE SON OF BATTLING MURDOCK SHOULD TAKE TO VIGOROUS TRAINING THE WAY A DUCK TAKES TO WATER! AND SO, IN THE MONTHS THAT FOLLOW, WHILE HIS DAD IS OUT OF TOWN ON THE BOXING CIRCUIT...

BAR BELLS

ROPE SKIPPING

CABLE PULL

THE BAG

ROWING MACHINE

THE BIKE

...UT, NO MATTER HOW HARD HE TRAINS, THE DETERMINED TEEN-AGER NEVER FORGETS THE GOAL HE HAS SET FOR HIMSELF...

HOW WERE THINGS AT SCHOOL WHILE I WAS AWAY, MATT? EVERY-THING ALL RIGHT, SON?

GUESS SO, DAD... IF YOU CALL STRAIGHT "A"S ALL RIGHT!

MATT, I KNOW HOW TOUGH IT'S BEEN FOR YOU WHILE THE OTHER KIDS WERE OUT PLAYIN' AND HAVIN' GOOD TIMES! BUT THE DAY WILL COME WHEN YOU'LL **THANK** ME, BOY! YOU'RE GONNA AMOUNT TO SOMETHING... JUST THE WAY YOUR MOTHER WOULD'VE **WANTED** YOU TO!

...UT, THERE IS ONE PROBLEM WHICH BATTLING MURDOCK KEEPS FROM HIS SON...

I HAVEN'T BEEN ABLE TO LAND A FIGHT IN WEEKS! I'M GETTIN' TOO OLD! NO MANAGER WILL TAKE ME! BUT I CAN'T LET MATT DOWN!

I'VE **GOT** TO KEEP FIGHTIN'! UNTIL HE GETS THROUGH COLLEGE! I **OWE** HIM THAT...FOR THE WAY HE'S WORKED ALL THESE YEARS!

FINALLY, IN DESPERATION, MURDOCK MAKES A FATAL DECISION...

LOOK, MURDOCK, YOU'RE ALL WASHED UP, AND YOU KNOW IT! THE ONLY GUY WHO'LL MANAGE A HAS-BEEN LIKE YOU IS THE **FIXER**!

THE **FIXER**! I ALWAYS SWORE TO MYSELF THAT I'D STEER CLEAR OF A GUY WITH **HIS** REPUTATION! BUT NOW I'VE GOT NO CHOICE! I **HAVE** TO GET A FIGHT!

XING

EXERCIZE ROOM

PRIVATE

7.

AND SO...

WELL, WELL, IF IT AIN'T BATTLING MURDOCK! TEN YEARS AGO YOU KICKED ME OUT OF YOUR DRESSING ROOM WHEN I OFFERED YOU A DEAL! BUT I KNEW YOU'D COME AROUND, SOONER OR LATER!

SURE, I'LL GET YA SOME FIGHTS! AND YOU WON'T HAVE TO TAKE A DIVE, EITHER! JUST BECAUSE I'M REALLY A SOFT-HEARTED FOOL! HERE, SIGN THIS CONTRACT!

WITH TREMBLING FINGERS, THE MIDDLE-AGED FIGHTER GRASPS THE PEN, AS A DROWNING MAN WOULD CLUTCH AT A STRAW! AND THEN...

THIS IS THE LUCKIEST DAY OF MY LIFE! NOW I'LL BE ABLE TO SEND MATT TO COLLEGE! I DON'T HAVE A THING TO WORRY ABOUT!

EXCITEDLY, THE JOYFUL PRIZE-FIGHTER RUSHES TO HIS APARTMENT ONLY TO FIND...

MATT! WAIT'L I TELL YOU TH NEWS! MATT.. HE'S NOT HERE

AS FATE WOULD HAVE IT, MATHEW MURDOCK, AT THAT VERY MOMENT, IS RETURNING FROM THE LIBRARY...TAKING THE MOST IMPORTANT FEW STEPS OF HIS ENTIRE LIFE!

GEE, YOU'D THINK SOMEONE WOULD HELP THAT BLIND MAN ACROSS THE STREET!

SAY, MISTER....CAN I GIVE YOU A HAND?

COZY CLEANERS

HE DIDN'T SEEM TO HEAR ME! HE MIGHT BE DEAF, TOO! SAY...THERE' A TRUCK TURNING THE CORNER... COMING TOWARDS HIM!

YANK... SLAM ON THE BRAKES! SOMEONE'S CROSSIN' IN FRONT OF US!

I CAN'T! SOMETHING'S WRONG! SHE WON'T STOP!

SCR/REECH!

AJAX ATOMIC LABS RADIO-ACTIVE MATERIALS DANGER

WITHOUT A MOMENT'S HESITATION... HIS SUPPLE MUSCLES RESPONDING TO THE EMERGENCY WITH THE SPEED OF THOUGHT... MATT MURDOCK HURTLES TOWARD THE SCENE OF IMPENDING DISASTER...

HE WON'T HAVE A CHANCE... UNLESS I CAN REACH HIM IN TIME!

THE SWIFT-MOVING TEEN-AGER HURLS THE UNSUSPECTING BLIND MAN OUT OF THE TRUCK'S PATH... BUT HE HIMSELF IS NOT SO FORTUNATE ...

OHHH...

HE SAVED THAT MAN'S LIFE!

MOST HEROIC ACT I'VE EVER SEEN!

BUT A CYLINDER FELL FROM THE TRUCK... IT STRUCK HIS FACE! IS... IS IT SOMETHING RADIOACTIVE??

DON'T JUST STAND THERE! SOMEONE CALL AN AMBULANCE!

ATOMIC LABS, INC. -TIVE MATERIALS -ANGER

LATER, AT MUNICIPAL HOSPITAL...

YOUR SON IS A VERY BRAVE LAD, MR. MURDOCK! YOU MUST TRY TO BE EQUALLY AS BRAVE IN THE DAYS AHEAD!

IF... IF ONLY IT HAD HAPPENED TO ME INSTEAD OF HIM! IF ONLY I HAD BEEN THERE!

DON'T, DAD! IT COULD BE WORSE! EVEN IF I DO LOSE MY SIGHT... AT LEAST I'M ALIVE!

AND, DAYS LATER, AFTER THE INJURED BOY RETURNS HOME ...

GOOD NEWS, MATT! THE DOCTOR'S REPORT SAYS THAT AN OPERATION MAY RESTORE YOUR SIGHT IN A FEW YEARS, AFTER THE TISSUES HAVE HEALED!

THAT'S GREAT, DAD! AND TILL THEN, DON'T WORRY! I'LL STILL KEEP UP MY STUDIES, USING BOOKS WRITTEN IN BRAILLE! I'LL GET MY DIPLOMA YET! YOU'LL SEE!!

9

BUT, IN THE DAYS THAT FOLLOW, MATT MURDOCK STUDIES *MORE* THAN THE WRITTEN WORD! HE BEGINS A STILL MORE INTENSIVE PROGRAM OF PHYSICAL EXERCISES...

I DON'T GET IT! EVER SINCE MY ACCIDENT, I SEEM ABLE TO DO EVERY-THING LOTS BETTER THAN BEFORE... EVEN WITHOUT MY SIGHT!

BONG!!

IT'S AS THOUGH NATURE MADE ALL MY SENSES FAR MORE POWER-FUL, TO COMPENSATE FOR MY BLINDNESS!

I WONDER... COULD THE *RADIO ACTIVE ELEMENT* WHICH STRUCK MY EYES HAVE ANYTHING TO DO WITH MY INCREASED POWERS? STRANGER THINGS HAVE BEEN KNOWN TO HAPPEN!

BUT, WHATEVER THE EXPLANATION, IT IS A SUPREMELY CONFIDENT, SELF-ASSURED MATT MURDOCK WHO FINALLY GRADUATES FROM HIGH SCHOOL AND IS EAGERLY ACCEPTED BY THE DIRECTOR OF ADMISSIONS OF STATE COLLEGE, WHERE WE FIND HIM SHARING A DORMITORY ROOM WITH HIS NEW BUDDY, FRANKLIN "FOGGY" NELSON...

D

MATT, YOU OL' HOUND DOG! HOW DO YOU DO IT? I STUDY LIKE A DEMON BUT *YOU* JUST BREEZE THROUGH THE COURSES WITH ALL THE TOP GRADES!

I GUESS MY DAD DESERVES THE CREDIT, FOGGY! HE HAD ME STUDY SO HARD WHEN I WAS YOUNGER, THAT IT ALL SEEMS TO COME EASY TO ME NOW!

AND, I WOULDN'T BE SURPRISED IF THAT RADIATION I ABSORBED IN THE ACCIDENT DOESN'T HAVE SOMETHING TO DO WITH IT, TOO! *EVERYTHING* SEEMS EASY FOR ME NOW! ALL MY SENSES ARE RAZOR SHARP!

"MY *HEARING* IS SO ACUTE, THAT I CAN TELL IF SOMEONE IS IN A ROOM WITH ME JUST BY HEARING THE *HEARTBEAT!*"

"AND I NEVER FORGET AN ODOR ONCE I *SMELL* IT! I COULD RECOGNIZE ANY GIRL BY HER PERFUME... OR ANY MAN BY HIS HAIR TONIC..."

"EVEN MY *FINGERS* HAVE BECOME INCREDIBLY SENSITIVE! I CAN TELL HOW MANY BULLETS ARE IN A GUN JUST BY THE WEIGHT OF THE BARREL."

"WHILE MY SENSE OF *TASTE* HAS BECOME SO HIGHLY DEVELOPED THAT I CAN TELL EXACTLY HOW MANY GRAINS OF SALT ARE ON A PIECE OF PRETZEL..."

10

BUT MY MOST *IMPORTANT* NEW ABILITY IS IN THE FORM OF A BUILT-IN *RADAR* THAT I SEEM TO HAVE DEVELOPED! IT ENABLES ME TO WALK ANYWHERE SAFELY, WITHOUT BUMPING INTO ANYTHING!"

I FEEL A STRANGE TINGLING SENSATION WHEN I APPROACH ANY SOLID OBSTACLE, WARNING ME WHICH WAY TO TURN!

PING! PING! PING!

SAY, SON... WANT ANY HELP CROSSIN' THE STREET?

NO THANKS! I CAN MAKE IT!

LITTLE DOES HE SUSPECT I CAN CROSS MORE SAFELY THAN *HE* CAN.. FOR I HAVE EVERY ONE OF MY RE-MAINING SENSES WORKING AT ABSOLUTE PEAK CAPACITY!

PING!

MEANWHILE, THE CAREER OF BATTLING MURDOCK TAKES A SURPRISING TURN...

MADISON SQ[U]
KID MURDOCK
[F]AVORITE
PEDRO GAR[CIA]
THURS. OCT. 10:00 P.M.
DAILY MES[SENGER]
MURDOCK K.O.S [HI]MS IN 9TH
SPORTS NE[WS]
MURDOCK 12TH KNO[CKOUT]

HERE'S YOUR DOUGH, MURDOCK! KEEP IT UP AND YOU MAY BE CHAMP, SOME-DAY!

I CAN'T BELIEVE IT, FIXER! IT ALL SEEMS LIKE SOME KINDA *MIRACLE!*

THEN, AFTER MURDOCK LEAVES...

WAIT'LL THE OLD FOOL FINDS OUT THAT ALL HIS FIGHTS WERE *SETUPS!* YOU PAID HIS OPPONENTS TO TAKE A DIVE!

SURE! I DID IT TO GIVE MURDOCK A BUILD-UP...TO DRAW THE CROWDS! BUT, HE'LL LEARN THE FACTS OF LIFE IN HIS *NEXT* FIGHT! THAT'S WHERE I GET *HIM* TO TAKE THE COUNT!

AND, A FEW DAYS BEFORE BATTLING MURDOCK'S LATEST FIGHT...

FOOTSTEPS! CAN TELL BY THE [W]EIGHT... THE [D]ISTANCE [B]ETWEEN [E]ACH... [I]T'S FOGGY [N]ELSON!

HEY, MATT! WAIT UP! I WANNA READ YOU THE SPORTS HEAD-LINE! IT'S ABOUT YOUR *DAD!*

HE'S FIGHTING DYNAMITE DAVIS TOMORROW NIGHT IN NEW YORK! HOW *ABOUT* THAT? WANNA GO??

I'VE ALREADY GOT THE TICKETS, FOGGY...ONE FOR EACH OF US!

I "READ" THE HEADLINE BEFORE ---JUST BY RUNNING MY FINGER OVER THE PAGE AND FEELING THE IMPRESSION OF THE INK!

DAILY CHRONICLE
"KID" MURDOCK TO FACE DAVIS, NO.2 CONTENDER!
SEMI-TI[TLE] [BOUT] AT GARDE[N] PROMISE[S] THRILLS

11.

AND SO THE NEXT NIGHT...

THE FIXER SAID I HAVE TO TAKE A DIVE IN THE FIRST ROUND TONIGHT!

...AND IN THIS CORNER, THE MIDDLE-AGED SENSATION... BATTLING MURDOCK!

BUT MY *BOY'S* HERE TONIGHT, TO ROOT FOR HIS *DAD!* I'VE ALWAYS TRAINED *HIM* TO DO HIS BEST... I CAN'T DISAPPOINT HIM NOW!

MURDOCK! YOU *FOOL!* TAKE IT *EASY!* WHAT ARE YOU *DOIN'?*

IF YOU'RE TRYIN' TO DOUBLE-CROSS ME YOU'LL LIVE TO REGRET IT! YOU'RE SUPPOSED TO *DIVE* NOW.. HEAR DIVE!

HE'S *WINNIN'*, MATT! YOUR DAD'S *PULVERIZING* HIM!

I *KNOW* IT! I CAN FOLLOW THE FIGHT PERFECTLY, BY HEARING THE SOUND OF EACH BLOW, EACH FOOT-STEP!

IT'S MY ONE CHANCE! ...MAYBE MY LAST CHANCE... TO DO SOMETHING TO MAKE MY SON *PROUD* OF ME! I'M NOT GONNA FAIL HIM! I'M GONNA WIN... DO YA HEAR... I'M *GONNA WIN!*

WHAM!

WHOP!

CALL IT A MIRACLE! CALL IT PURE WILL POWER!... SHEER DETERMINATION! CALL IT WHAT YOU WILL, BUT A FEW SECONDS LATER...

THE WINNAH... BATTLING MURDOCK!!

AND THEN, IN THE DRESSING ROOM...

YOU *DID* IT, DAD! YOU PROVED THAT *NOTHING'S* IMPOSSIBLE IF A MAN HAS THE COURAGE! IF A MAN'S NOT *AFRAID!!*

I WANTED YOU TO BE PROUD OF ME, MATT... MY SON!

BUT, IN THE BACK SEAT OF A DARK SEDAN WHICH QUIETLY PULLS AWAY FROM THE STADIUM.

NOBODY DOUBLE-CROSSES THE FIXER! YOU KNOW WHAT TO DO, SLADE!

YEAH, BOSS... I KNOW WHAT TO DO!

FEW MINUTES LATER, AS MATT'S HAPPY FATHER LEAVES THE GYM...

NO MATTER WHAT THE FIXER DOES, I WON'T CARE! MY SON IS *PROUD* OF ME! NOTHING CAN EVER CHANGE THAT NOW!

SUDDENLY, THE SHARP, EXPLOSIVE SOUND OF A GUN SHOT DESTROYS THE SILENCE OF NIGHT, AND ENDS ONE MAN'S REVERIE, FOREVER!

CRACK!

WITHIN SECONDS...

IT'S *BATTLING MURDOCK!* HE WON THE BIG FIGHT TONIGHT!

SOMEBODY MUST HAVE BEEN AWFULLY SORE ABOUT HIS VICTORY! AND WE'RE NOT GOING TO REST UNTIL WE FIND OUT *WHO!!*

NOTHING I CAN DO FOR HIM... IT'S TOO LATE!

LATER, AFTER A GRIEVING MATT MURDOCK HAS HEARD THE TRAGIC NEWS...

YOU'VE GOTTA SNAP OUT OF IT, MATT! PULL YOURSELF TOGETHER, FELLA! THAT'S WHAT YOUR DAD WOULD HAVE WANTED!

WE'LL BE GRADUATING SOON, AND MY DAD'S SETTING ME UP IN A LAW OFFICE! I WANT YOU TO JOIN ME, MATT...AS MY PARTNER!

FINALLY...THE BIG DAY ARRIVES...GRADUATION...

MATTHEW MURDOCK, I AM ESPECIALLY PROUD TO CONGRATULATE YOU FOR BEING CHOSEN CLASS VALEDICTORIAN! YOU HAVE PROVEN THAT AN ALERT MIND AND A STRONG WILL CAN CONQUER ANY OBSTACLES!

THANK YOU, SIR!

AND HE'S GONNA BE MY PARTNER! BOY! CAN I PICK 'EM!

THE NEXT DAY, IN NEW YORK...

WE'RE IN *BUSINESS*, MATT! WITH YOUR BRAINS AND MY DAD'S MONEY, *NOTHING'LL* STOP US!

C'MON IN AND MEET THE SECRETARY I HIRED!

NELSON AND MURDOCK

- ATTORNEYS AT LAW -

ENTER

MY NAME IS KAREN PAGE, MR. MURDOCK! I HOPE YOU'LL BE PLEASED WITH ME!

HER VOICE IS LIKE MUSIC! FROM THE SOUND, SHE'S FIVE-FEET-FOUR, YOUNG, AND I *KNOW* SHE'S LOVELY!

LATER THAT NIGHT, IN THE FURNISHED ROOM MATT HAS RENTED NEAR THE OFFICE...

I'LL *NEVER* BE ABLE TO CONCENTRATE ON MY LAW WORK UNTIL DAD'S MURDERER IS FINALLY BROUGHT TO JUSTICE! BUT YEARS AGO I PROMISED DAD THAT MATT MURDOCK WOULD USE HIS *HEAD*... NEVER BECOME A FIGHTER.. NEVER DEPEND ON MY STRENGTH, THE WAY *DAD* DID!

13.

I CAN'T BREAK THAT PROMISE I MADE! AND YET, WITH MY AGILITY, MY EXTRA-SHARP SENSES, THERE IS SO *MUCH* I COULD DO! I CAN'T LET ALL MY POWERS GO TO WASTE!

WAIT! I HAVE IT!

SNAP!

I'LL SEE TO IT THAT MATT MURDOCK NEVER *DOES* RESORT TO FORCE...BUT SOMEBODY *ELSE* WILL...! SOMEBODY TOTALLY *DIFFERENT* FROM MATT MURDOCK... ALL I NEED ARE SOME OLD SHIRTS WHICH I CAN STITCH TOGETHER!

I'M NO BETSY ROSS, BUT I SHOULD BE ABLE TO HANDLE THIS! LUCKY MY TOUCH IS SO SENSITIVE!

I CAN EVEN BLEND THE *COLORS*, FOR EACH COLORED FABRIC HAS A DIFFERENT *FEEL* TO ME!

A FEW HOURS LATER...

THERE! WHENEVER I DON THIS COSTUME, I'LL NO LONGER *BE* MATT MURDOCK! BUT I'LL NEED A *NEW* NAME! WHAT IF THE KIDS IN THE OLD NEIGHBORHOOD COULD SEE ME NOW!! THE KIDS WHO TAUNTED ME...CALLED ME "DAREDEVIL"! *WAIT!* THAT'S *IT!!*

"DAREDEVIL" THEY CALLED ME... BUT THEY MEANT IT AS AN INSULT! WELL, THAT'S WHO I'LL *BE*... THE NAME IS *PERFECT!*

EVEN THOUGH I DON'T *NEED* IT, I'LL CONTINUE TO CARRY A CANE AS MATT MURDOCK! MMM...THAT GIVES ME ANOTHER IDEA! THAT CANE WOULD MAKE A GREAT WEAPON FOR *DAREDEVIL!*

THE COSTUME IS TIGHT ENOUGH TO WEAR UNDER MY CLOTHES IF NEED BE I'LL JUST MAKE A FEW FINISHING TOUCHES ON THE HEADPIECE! WHEN I'M THROUGH, *DAREDEVIL* WILL BE RECOGNIZED *ANYWHERE!!*

THROUGH THE LONG NIGHT, THE UNSEEING MAN WORKS... HIS SUPER-SENSITIVE FINGERS MOLDING AND MANIPULATING HIS CANE FAR MORE PRECISELY THAN ANY NORMAL CRAFTSMAN MIGHT DO IT!

FLEXI HAND

HINGE

I'LL HINGE IT IN THE MIDDLE... DESIGN A SHEATH FOR IT...IT'LL BE THE PERFECT ALL-PURPOSE WEAPON!

I WANT TO KNOW WHAT ARRANGEMENT YOU HAD WITH BATTLING MURDOCK!

BATTLING MURDOCK!! WHAT'S THAT TO YOU??! IT AIN'T HEALTHY TO MENTION HIM AROUND HERE!

HE MUST KNOW SOMETHING, BOSS! I'LL TAKE CARE OF HIM!

THE SOUND OF A SUIT JACKET BEING DRAWN ASIDE! FINGERS TOUCHING A METAL OBJECT! MUST BE A GUN BUTT...IN A SHOULDER HOLSTER!

THE SOUND OF HIS BREATHING... THE TELLTALE CLICK OF THE PISTOL'S SAFETY RELEASE... ARE ALL I NEED HEAR TO PINPOINT MY TARGET!

...AND THE ALMOST INAUDIBLE SOUND OF MY CANE CUTTING THROUGH THE AIR I LIKE A LOUD RADAR BEEP TO MY SUPER SENSITIVE EARS!

I WAS RIGHT ALL THE TIME! MY SENSES ARE SO ULTRA-KEEN THAT I CAN DO ANYTHING A MAN WITH EYESIGHT CAN...AND DO IT BETTER!!

I'LL SNEAK UP ON HIM FROM BEHIND AND...HEY! HE SWUNG AROUND JUST IN TIME!

HOW'D YOU KNOW I WAS BEHIND YOU?!

THAT'S MY SECRET, PAL!

NO MATTER HOW SOFTLY HE CREPT UP BEHIND ME, HIS MUFFLED FOOTSTEPS SOUNDED LIKE HEAVY DRUM BEATS TO ME!!

RAPID FOOTSTEPS HURRYING AWAY FROM ME! HE'S TRYING TO ESCAPE!

HOLD IT, SPEEDY! I HAVEN'T DISMISSED THE CLA YET!!

HOW DOES HE DO IT? H DOESN'T MIS A TRICK!

NOW LET'S ALL SETTLE DOWN FOR A NICE TALK... UNLESS YOU'D LIKE ANOTHER SESSION WITH ME!

LOOK, YOU...

QUIET! I'LL HANDLE THIS! I'M STILL THE BOSS!

SLAM!

MISTER, WHOEVER YOU ARE...YOU'RE IN A MESS OF TROUBLE! YOU'RE NOT GETTIN' AWAY WITH COMIN' HERE AND ROUGHING US UP! WE GOT LAWS TO PROTECT INNOCENT PEOPLE! SAM, CALL THE COPS!!

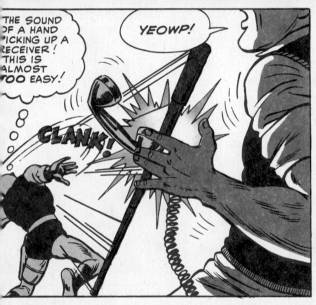

THE SOUND OF A HAND PICKING UP A RECEIVER! THIS IS ALMOST TOO EASY!

YEOWP!

CLANK!

FIXER, I SUSPECT YOU WERE RESPONSIBLE FOR THE DEATH OF BATTLING MURDOCK! WHY DON'T YOU CONFESS NOW AND SAVE US ALL A LOT OF TROUBLE!?

YOU'RE NUTS! I HAD NOTHIN' TO DO WITH IT! I GOT A PERFECT ALIBI!

I HAVE ANOTHER POWER I WASN'T EVEN AWARE OF! I CAN HEAR HIS PULSE RATE! IT'S SPEEDING UP, INDICATING HE'S LYING! MY SUPER-SENSE OF HEARING IS LIKE A BUILT-IN LIE DETECTOR!

MAYBE YOU DO HAVE AN ALIBI! MAYBE YOURS WASN'T THE FINGER THAT SQUEEZED THE TRIGGER! BUT YOU GAVE THE ORDER... DIDN'T YOU??

NO! NO! STAY BACK!! STOP HIM, YOU GUYS... DON'T LET 'IM GET ME!

17.

HE KNOWS TOO MUCH!! HE MIGHT EVEN KNOW *I'M* THE MURDERER! CAN'T TAKE ANY CHANCES!

SO INTENT IS DAREDEVIL UPON LISTENING TO THE FIXER'S PULSE RATE, TO DETERMINE IF HE IS THE GUILTY MAN, THAT HIS ULTRA-SHARP HEARING SENSE REACTS A FRACTION OF A SECOND TOO SLOW, AND...

IT WAS *ME*... BUT YOU'LL NEVER BE ABLE TO *DO* ANYTHING ABOUT IT!

BEHIND ME!! SOMEONE... OHHH!

A NORMAL MAN, WITH ALL HIS SENSES, MIGHT BE DOOMED IN SUCH A SITUATION! BUT, THE MOMENT THE FEARLESS *DAREDEVIL* FEELS HIMSELF HURTLING INTO SPACE, HIS SUPER-KEEN EARS CATCH THE RUSTLING OF A FLAG, AS HIS LIGHTNING-FAST REFLEXES GO INTO ACTION...

A FLAGPOLE ALONGSIDE ME... ONLY ONE CHANCE!!

PRESSING THE HIDDEN STUD WHICH RELEASES HIS CANE HANDLE AT THE SAME SPLIT SECOND AS HE LUNGES OUT, HE STOPS HIS FALL IN MIDAIR!!

GOT IT!!

FROM HERE ON IN, IT'S ALL A BREEZE!

NOW THEN, GENTS... WHERE *WERE* WE??

HE'S BACK!!

WHUMP!

MEANWHILE, AT THE OTHER SIDE OF TOWN...

FUNNY, MATT DOESN'T ANSWER! MAYBE HE'S STILL ASLEEP! OH... THE DOOR'S OPEN!

HEY, LAZYBONES! I THOUGHT I'D SEE IF YOU *NEED* ANYTHING, AND... MATT?? HE'S *GONE!*

GOSH, I WISH HE'D *CALLED* ME! I HATE TO THINK OF POOR MATT WALKING AROUND TOWN ALL ALONE, WITH ALL THE TRAFFIC IN NEW YORK!

I'LL GO UP TO THE OFFICE...MAYBE HE DECIDED TO COME HERE AND GET FAMILIAR WITH THE PLACE BEFORE STARTING WORK ON MONDAY!

BUT, ENTERING THE NEW OFFICE, FOGGY FINDS IT UNOCCUPIED, EXCEPT FOR THE MOST DECORATIVE ACCESSORY...

KAREN! TODAY'S YOUR DAY OFF!

I KNOW, MR. NELSON! BUT I'M A STRANGER IN NEW YORK, AND HAD NO ONE TO VISIT, SO I THOUGHT I'D TIDY UP THE OFFICE WHILE I HAD A CHANCE! IS MR. MURDOCK WITH YOU?

NO! MATTER OF FACT, I HOPED HE'D BE HERE! I DON'T LIKE HIM WANDERING AROUND TOWN ALONE!

I UNDERSTAND! WHAT A PITY SUCH A WONDERFUL, HANDSOME MAN IS SO HANDI-CAPPED!

WOW! I'D SURE LIKE TO HEAR HER TALK ABOUT ME IN THAT ADORING TONE OF VOICE!

DON'T LET HIS BLINDNESS FOOL YOU, KAREN! HE'S STILL THE SMARTEST, MOST CAPABLE, MOST COURAGEOUS FELLA I KNOW! HE DOESN'T EVEN SEEM TO MIND NOT SEEING!

THERE'S SOMETHING ABOUT HIM THAT MAKES A GIRL WANT TO TAKE HIM IN HER ARMS AND... OH, I'M SORRY, MR. NELSON! I HAD NO RIGHT TO SPEAK THAT WAY! IT'S JUST THAT HE SEEMS TO NEED SOME-ONE TO LOOK AFTER HIM!

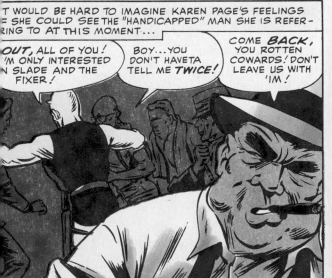

IT WOULD BE HARD TO IMAGINE KAREN PAGE'S FEELINGS IF SHE COULD SEE THE "HANDICAPPED" MAN SHE IS REFER-RING TO AT THIS MOMENT...

OUT, ALL OF YOU! I'M ONLY INTERESTED IN SLADE AND THE FIXER!

BOY...YOU DON'T HAVETA TELL ME TWICE!

COME BACK, YOU ROTTEN COWARDS! DON'T LEAVE US WITH 'IM!

NOW, YOU TWO, I'VE LEARNED WHAT I WANTED! SLADE ACTUALLY DID THE SHOOTING, BUT YOU GAVE THE ORDER!

WHAT GOOD'LL IT DO YOU?? YOU CAN'T PROVE IT!

YEAH! WHERE'S YOUR EVIDENCE??

19.

NOW FOR MY *FINAL* BLUFF! THEY'RE SO WORRIED NOW, THEY'LL BELIEVE *ANYTHING!*

RIGHT *HERE!* I HAVE A MINIATURE TAPE RECORDER CONCEALED IN MY BILLY CLUB! IT'LL TELL THE POLICE ALL THEY NEED TO KNOW!

HE'S *GOT* US!

THEN, BEFORE DAREDEVIL CAN MAKE A MOVE, THE FIXER TRIES ONE LAST, DESPERATE MANEUVER...

QUICK, SLADE...*RUN!* BEFORE HE CAN GET HIS BALANCE!

OHHH..

MY *ARM!* I WRENCHED IT! I WAS A FOOL FOR BEING SO OVERCONFIDENT! I SHOULD HAVE *KNOWN* THEY'D MAKE ONE FINAL TRY TO ESCAPE!

THEY CAN'T HAVE GOTTEN *FAR!* I'LL GET THEM *YET!*

BUT, RACING AROUND THE CORNER, SLADE AND THE FIXER QUICKLY MINGLE WITH THE SATURDAY AFTERNOON SHOPPING CROWD.

HE'LL NEVER FIND US NOW, IN THE MIDDLE OF THIS CROWD!

JUST THE SAME, KEEP MOVING! THERE'S NO TELLIN' *WHAT* THAT GUY CAN DO!

MEANWHILE...

I CAN STILL SMELL THE TRACES OF THE FIXER'S CIGAR SMOKE! I CAN FOLLOW THE SCENT LIKE A BLOODHOUND...BUT I'LL BE ABLE TO GET AROUND EASIER IN THE CROWD *WITHOUT* A COSTUME!!

AND SO BEGINS ONE OF THE STRANGEST PURSUITS ON RECORD, AS A MAN WITHOUT SIGHT UNERRINGLY MAKES HIS WAY THROUGH A CROWDED AVENUE, ON THE TRAIL OF TWO KILLERS!

I'M GLAD HIS CIGAR IS A STRONG ONE! HE MIGHT AS WELL BE *TELLING* ME WHERE HE IS...BUT HE DOESN'T *KNOW* IT!!

200

WITHIN MINUTES, THE GRACEFUL, SUPPLE FIGURE OF MATT MURDOCK HAS KNIFED THROUGH THE UNSUSPECTING CROWD LIKE A SHADOWY WRAITH, AND THEN...

I HOPE THEY'RE STAYING TOGETHER! I WANT TO BRING THEM *BOTH* TO JUSTICE! THE CIGAR SCENT IS STRONGER NOW...I'M ALMOST UP TO THEM!

SLOW DOWN, SLADE! WE'RE NOWHERE IN SIGHT!

GUESS YOU'RE RIGHT! NO ONE NEAR US NOW BUT THAT BLIND GUY! WE'VE LOST 'IM FOR SURE!

C'MON, WE'LL DUCK INTO THAT SUBWAY STATION ACROSS THE STREET AND GET OFF AT PENN STATION! WE'LL BE OUTTA TOWN IN AN HOUR!

THAT'S WHAT *THEY* THINK!

HEY! DIDJA SEE HOW FAST THAT BLIND GUY PUSHED PAST US?

WHO CARES? WE GOT OUR *OWN* PROBLEMS!

BUT UNKNOWN TO THE FLEEING DUO, THEIR PROBLEMS ARE JUST *BEGINNING*! FOR, DIRECTLY *AHEAD* OF THEM...

THEIR FOOTSTEPS ARE GETTING CLOSER! I'LL JUST MAKE IT!!

GOING SOMEWHERE, BOYS?!

IT'S *HIM*!!

IT...IT AIN'T *POSSIBLE*!

SEPARATE! HE CAN'T GET US *BOTH*!!

I WAS *AFRAID* THEY'D TRY THAT!

I CAN TELL BY THE UNBROKEN SOUND OF SLADE'S FOOTSTEPS, THERE'S NO ONE BETWEEN US! ...SO IT'S SAFE TO THROW MY CANE!

GOOD! HE'S TACKLING *SLADE*! THAT MEANS *I'LL* ESCAPE!

21.

DON'T YOU KNOW ENOUGH TO STAY WHERE I LEFT YOU??

...HH!!

NOW FOR MY LAST BLUFF!

THE FIXER JUST TOLD US EVERYTHING, SLADE! HE'S INNOCENT! YOU ARE MURDOCK'S MURDERER!

THE DIRTY CRUMB! HE'S NOT GONNA WIGGLE OUT OF THIS! HE'S AS GUILTY AS I AM! I ONLY PULLED THE TRIGGER.. BUT HE GAVE THE ORDERS!

HEAR ENOUGH, BOYS??

WE SURE DID! BUT...

WAIT! WHO ARE YOU?

THE NAME'S DAREDEVIL ... REMEMBER IT! YOU'LL BE HEARING IT AGAIN... I PROMISE!!

NOT LONG AFTERWARDS...

MATT! SAY, I WAS WORRIED ABOUT YOU, FELLA! WHERE'VE YOU BEEN?

JUST OUT FOR A WALK, FOGGY! I'D HAVE BEEN HERE SOONER, BUT AS YOU KNOW... I CAN'T GET AROUND TOO FAST!

WE JUST HAD A CALL, MR. MURDOCK! AN ACCUSED MURDERER, NAMED SLADE ... HE WANTED TO KNOW IF WE'D DEFEND HIM!

BUT I TURNED HIM DOWN! FROM THE POLICE REPORT, I WAS CONVINCED HE'S GUILTY! HOPE YOU DON'T MIND, MATT!

MIND??

NO! I DON'T MIND AT ALL! NOT A BIT! NOT ONE SINGLE BIT!

DAD, WHEREVER YOU ARE ... I KINDA HOPE YOU'RE RESTING EASIER NOW!

When we said Daredevil had changed since his origin story, we weren't just whistlin' Dixie. To show you the amazing extent of that change, we now present a totally updated version of ol' Hornhead, as seen in his famous issue #232.

Y'know, there was a period of time, years after we introduced the adventures of Matt Murdock to a gratifyingly grateful public, when his stories seemed to get darker and darker, grittier and grittier. It was as though the savagery of the world in which he lived was actually affecting his life and the lives of those around him.

The story that follows depicts Daredevil's most ubiquitous enemy, the super-rich, super-powerful, super-evil Kingpin, who is so obsessed with our hero's total destruction that he unleashes the most uncontrollable, most maniacal, most bloodthirsty assassin of all, with just one objective—destroy Matt Murdock—no matter how many other lives must go down with him!

It's a stark and savage tale, not for the faint-hearted. But it's also the tale of a man who comes back—a fighter who can't be kept down—a hero in a red costume who shows once again that courage and valor are not only for the sighted!

You've probably guessed by now that Matt Murdock is one of Marvel's all-time favorite heroes. Despite his handicap, despite his vulnerability, he has a nobility of spirit that won't ever let him quit. He's a hero for our time, a hero for us all.

He's Daredevil—the Man Without Fear!

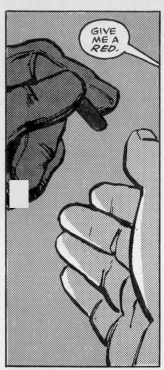

GIVE ME A *RED.*

OUR *BOYS*-- OUR *BOYS*--

NUKE-- THAT'S *WRONG,* BOY, YOU'VE GOT IT *WRONG.*

YOU ARE *NOT* IN *VIETNAM*--

-- YOU ARE *NOT* LOOKING FOR *MIAS.*

THIS IS *NICARAGUA*--

BETSY-- FORGOT TO SET *BETSY*--

GOOD COUNT-- BEST *YET*--

--I'LL *TOP* IT FOR YOU, *COLONEL.*

YOU'LL GET YOUR *CHANCE,* BOY.

THERE'S A *LOT* OF THEM DOWN THERE.

AND THEY'RE *HOLDING*-- OUR *BOYS*--

BETSY HUMS AS THE *RED* STARTS COMING IN AROUND THE EDGES AND THE COLONEL'S *VOICE* STOPS SLOWING THINGS *DOWN.*

--OUR BOYS--

BETSY, SHE KNOWS WHAT TO DO. THE PROGRAM'S ALL SET.

STAGE ONE.

NAPALM.

SHE KNOWS WHAT TO DO.

SHE KEEPS THE COUNT.

005

RED'S KICKING IN BUT GOOD NOW-- ADRENALIN RUSH LIKE A ROCKET BLAST--

BRAKABRAK

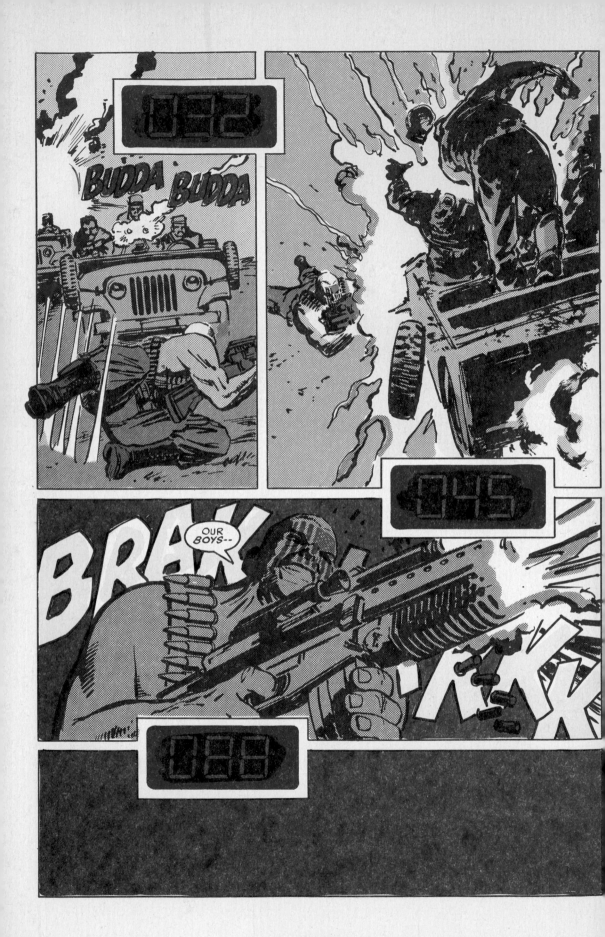

GIVE ME A *WHITE*.

WHERE *NEXT*?

YOU'RE NOT GOING TO *BELIEVE* THIS, BOY.

YOU'RE HOPPING A *CIVILIAN* PLANE. GOING *STATESIDE*. NEW YORK.

ORDER CAME DOWN WHILE YOU WERE MOPPING *UP*. STRAIGHT FROM THE *GENERAL*.

GENERAL SEEMS TO HAVE GOTTEN HIMSELF SOME NEW *FRIENDS*.

NEW YORK-- AMERICA...

AMERICA.

...SO *GLAD* YOU COULD TAKE MY *CALL*, MR. FISK... AH...JUST THOUGHT YOU'D BE GLAD TO *KNOW*...

...AH...*NUKE*--I MEAN AGENT *SIMPSON*...WELL, HE'S *EN ROUTE*, MR. FISK. COMING YOUR *WAY*, JUST LIKE YOU...LIKE YOU *WANTED*...

...I HAVE... AH...*DELIVERED THE GOODS*, MR. FISK...AND...AND, WELL...

...WELL, I'M *WAITING* FOR THE GOODS YOU PROMISED *ME*...

NUKE.

SUCH A SIMPLE TERM. SO DIRECT.

AND NOW THE KINGPIN OF CRIME WILL AIM THIS NUKE AT THE MAN HE IS LEARNING TO HATE.

THE MAN HE IS LEARNING TO FEAR.

MURDOCK.

KAREN PAGE TRIES TO SCREAM BUT THE ONLY SOUND SHE CAN MAKE IS A DRY SUCKING--

--SUCKING. SHE THINKS OF WHAT SHE LEARNED IN COLLEGE --IN SCIENCE CLASS--WHAT SHE LEARNED ABOUT BLACK HOLES--

--STARS THAT COLLAPSE IN ON THEMSELVES AND STOP SHINING--COLLAPSE UNTIL THERE'S NOTHING LEFT LESS THAN NOTHING--

--JUST A HOLE THAT SUCKS EVERYTHING IN AND TAKES IT NOWHERE-- JUST SUCKS AND SUCKS--

--AND SHE'D GO SHE'D DISAPPEAR AND IT WOULDN'T MATTER--BUT HIS ARMS ARE STRONG AND HE HOLDS HER HERE ON EARTH--

--THINK OF HIM--THINK OF MATT MURDOCK--

--MATT--THEY ALMOST GOT MARRIED ONCE BEFORE SHE WENT FOR THE MOVIES--BEFORE SHE LEFT HIM TO BECOME A STAR--

--AND THE MOVIES GOT WORSE AND WORSE AND PIECE BY PIECE KAREN PAGE SOLD HER SOUL--

--THE LAST PIECE SHE SOLD FOR A SHOT OF HEROIN-- A LOUSY FIX FOR THE LOUSY JUNKIE SHE'D BECOME--

--THE LAST PIECE OF HER-- MATT--SHE SOLD MATT OUT-- TOLD A PUSHER THAT MATT IS DAREDEVIL--

--AND THE PUSHER SOLD THAT TO MATT'S ENEMIES--AND THEY TOOK MATT'S HOME AND CAREER AND EVERYTHING--

--NO-- NOT EVERYTHING--

--"NOTHING," HE'D SAID, MATT DID, WHEN SHE TOLD HIM WHAT SHE'D DONE--

--"I'VE LOST NOTHING," MATT SAID, AND LAUGHED LIKE A BOY--

--AND KAREN DIDN'T UNDER-STAND--AND MATT KISSED HER--

--AND HELD HER...

...AND KNOWS EXACTLY WHAT TO SAY AND WHEN TO MAKE HER EAT AND HOW TO TOUCH THE MUSCLES IN HER BACK TO MAKE HER SLEEP...

...THAT'S HIS SENSES. HIS CRAZY SENSES.

HE WAS A BOY. IT WAS BEFORE SHE MET HIM. HE WAS BLINDED BY RADIATION OR SOMETHING AND HIS REMAINING SENSES BECAME SUPERHUMAN.

SHE NEVER TOLD THEM ABOUT THE SENSES.

AND SHE NEVER TOLD THEM--ABOUT THE MAN.

STAN LEE presents

GOD AND COUNTRY

by FRANK MILLER and DAVID MAZZUCCHELLI

MAX SCHEELE
COLORS

JOE ROSEN
LETTERS

RALPH MACCHIO
EDITOR

JIM SHOOTER
EDITOR IN CHIEF

From the length of my ENTOURAGE, you'd think I'm a visiting DIGNITARY-- or a crook.

I'm NEITHER. My name is BEN URICH. I'm a REPORTER.

These days, I'm a reporter in the HOT SEAT-- investigating the city's top CRIMINAL-- the KINGPIN-- and trying to stay ALIVE all the while.

Staying ALIVE involves finding the Kingpin's ENEMY-- and my FRIEND. A man named MATT MURDOCK who has a lot of SECRETS and seems to have grown MORE.

Like where he IS.

YOU'VE BEEN CLOSE TO MURDOCK SINCE COLLEGE, HAVEN'T YOU, MR. NELSON?

CLOSE AS ANYBODY, I GUESS.

LOOK, I'LL ONLY TALK IF IT'S GOING TO HELP MATT, MR. URICH. I MEAN, SUPPOSE HE DOESN'T WANT TO BE FOUND...

YOU THINK IT'S A GOOD IDEA FOR A BLIND MAN TO WANDER OFF ALONE?

NO, BUT...

But MATT is no ORDINARY blind man. I know that, NELSON. Do YOU?

...OKAY, MR. URICH, I'LL TRUST YOU. MATT ALWAYS SPOKE WELL OF YOU AND THAT'S GOOD ENOUGH FOR ME.

ALL OF THOSE CHARGES AGAINST HIM ARE FALSE-- AND YOU CAN BET I'LL HAVE HIS APPEAL READY, JUST AS SOON AS THIS WHOLE MESS GETS UNTANGLED. BUT... WELL...

...WELL, EVER SINCE OUR LAW FIRM WENT UNDER -- AND EVEN BEFORE-- MATT'S BEEN...

...WELL, I SPOKE WITH HIM-- I MEAN, HE *PHONED* ME, AFTER HIS *HOUSE* BLEW UP, AND... HE SOUNDED VERY *CONFUSED*...

HE SOUNDED *CRAZY*, MR. NELSON. I'VE SPOKEN WITH HIM *MYSELF*.

I WOULDN'T GO SO FAR AS TO SAY *THAT*. MATT'S ALWAYS BEEN KIND OF *HIGH STRUNG*. I MEAN, YOU JUST CAN'T ALWAYS *WORRY*...

...I'M SURE HE'LL BE ...LOOK, LET ME SHOW YOU WHAT I'VE GOT WORKED UP FOR THE *APPEAL*.

OF COURSE, THERE'S STILL A LOT OF *EVIDENCE* TO-- WHOOPS--

DARN IT-- I'M SUCH A--

WHERE DID YOU GET THESE *PHOTOS?*

GLORI...UM ...GLORIANNA O'BREEN... SHE'S--

MATT'S GIRLFRIEND? HE NEVER *TOLD* ME. BUT THEN, HE WOULDN'T *KNOW*...

WILL YOU BE *SEEING* HER ANY TIME SOON?

YEAH. YEAH. I...UM... I'LL BE SEEING HER *TONIGHT*...

ASK HER TO CALL ME. PLEASE.

IT'S NOT LIKE SHE'S SOME FINE ART *GALLERY FLIRT* LOOKING TO COURT THE *WINE* AND *CHEESE* CROWD AND TALK ABOUT HER *CHILDHOOD* AS IF IT WERE WORTH THE *TELLING.*

LIKE THAT *MAN* THERE SO *BIG* AND *TOUGH* AND JUST THE *SAME* HOLDING ONTO THAT *JACKHAMMER* FOR DEAR LIFE--

--JUST LEAPED OUT AND *BEGGED* TO BE TAKEN.

SHE'S JUST GOT *EYES,* IS ALL. AND THINGS KEEP LEAPING *OUT* AT HER.

IT'S ALMOST *ROBBERY.* THINKS GLORIANNA O'BREEN.

GIVE ME A *BLUE.*

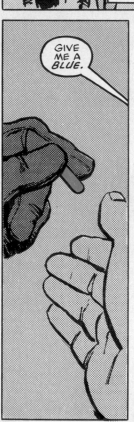

UM...*EXCUSE* ME, SIR--ABOUT THAT *BEER* YOU ORDERED--

--WE DON'T *HAVE* THE BRAND YOU *ASKED* FOR-- IT ISN'T *MADE* ANYMORE-- SO WE *SUBSTITUTED* --

AAAA--

THIS BRAND-- WHERE WAS IT *BREWED?*

M--MILWAUKEE.

DON'T *WORRY,* BOY, IT'S *AMERICAN.*

ALL RIGHT. ALL RIGHT.

TROUBLE, MR. FISK. IT'S YOUR GIRL *LOIS*.

SINCE SHE WAS *APPREHENDED* TRYING TO MURDER BEN URICH'S *WIFE*--SHE'S BEEN *TALKING*. ABOUT *YOU*.

THE *DISTRICT ATTORNEY* HAS AGREED TO *REDUCED* CHARGES IN EXCHANGE FOR HER TURNING *STATE'S EVIDENCE*.

I'M AFRAID THAT'S NOT *ALL*. EVER SINCE *URICH* GOT ON YOUR *CASE*, HE'S BEEN *COZY* WITH THE D.A.--

--AND NOW HE'S LANDED AN *INTERVIEW* WITH LOIS.

COMMISSIONER...YOU WILL SEE TO IT THAT OFFICER *COOGAN* IS ON DUTY AT THE TIME OF THE INTERVIEW.

THAT IS ALL.

MR. *FISK*-- ABOUT THOSE *PICTURES*...

EMBARRASSING, AREN'T THEY, COMMISSIONER? SUCH AN *ORDINARY* COCKTAIL WAITRESS. YOUR WIFE WOULD BE *INSULTED*.

YOU NEED NOT *WORRY*, MY FRIEND. I WILL KEEP THE PHOTOS *SAFE*.

QUITE *SAFE*.

AW, GLORI, I WAS *COUNTING* ON TONIGHT...WHAT? A NEW *JOB*?...

THE *DAILY BUGLE*. NO *KIDDING*. I GUESS URICH WAS *SERIOUS*. I DIDN'T KNOW *YOU* WERE...

...NO, HONEY, I DIDN'T MEAN ANYTHING BY THAT...

...IT'S JUST THAT YOUR *PHOTOGRAPHY* NEVER... I MEAN, YOU NEVER *TALKED* ABOUT IT...NO, NO-- MORE LIKE A *HOBBY*...

...YES, I GUESS I *DO* KNOW NOW... OF *COURSE* I'M HAPPY FOR YOU, HONEY...

...WELL, I JUST WANTED TO *TALK* TO YOU...IT'S THIS *JOB*. IT...

...OH, FOR *CORPORATE* WORK IT'S OKAY...AND THE *PAY* IS GREAT... BUT...

...BUT SOME OF THE *WORK* THEY DO HERE...I'M NOT SURE IT'S *LEGITIMATE*...

HE'D BEEN UP ALL NIGHT WITH HER.

IT WAS EARLY IN THE MORNING AND HE BOUGHT A RAZOR AND WAS SHAVING, HE WAS ABOUT TO GO TO WORK--

-- HE ACTUALLY LIKES THAT JOB HE FOUND --

-- WHEN KAREN FELL ASLEEP.

SHE WOKE ALONE BUT THAT'S OKAY, NOW. THE WORST IS OVER, FOR ME IT'S OVER, SHE THINKS--

--BUT MATT--WHAT'S HE GOING THROUGH?

AND WHAT'S HE WAITING FOR?

NIGHT AFTER NIGHT HE KEEPS TOUCHING THE COSTUME AND PACING AND FROWNING LIKE A LITTLE KID WHO HAS TO STAY AFTER CLASS. WHY DOESN'T HE JUST PUT THE THING ON AND DANCE ACROSS THE BUILDINGS--HE'S LIKE A GOD WHEN HE DOES THAT-- HE'S ACHING FOR IT...

WE'VE BOTH CHANGED, MATT. I USED TO WORRY WHEN YOU DID PUT IT ON. BUT NOW...

...YOU'RE WARM AND SWEET AND STRONG BUT THERE'S SOME- THING...SOMETHING NEW...

...SOMETHING COLD AND HARD. SOME- THING WAITING.

SOMETHING FRIGHTENING.

HE'S STILL MATT, SHE THINKS, AND SLEEPS.

It's the city JAIL. They call it the TOMBS. They have their REASONS.

SAVE YOUR *FILM*, GLORI. *LOCATION* SHOTS YOU CAN SELL TO *TOURISTS*. GET THE *PEOPLE*-- AND GET THE *ACTION*. THAT'S WHAT *STORIES* ARE MADE OF.

YOU'VE EXPLAINED IT WELL *ENOUGH*, MR. URICH.

SHOULDN'T GET *TESTY* WITH URICH, GLOR-- *JAMESON* MADE HIM *RESPONSIBLE* FOR YOU. AND *URICH*, HE'S A REAL *LONER*. DOESN'T EVEN LIKE HAVING THE *COP* ALONG. KLIK

DRIVES HIM *CRAZY* HAVING *ME*. BUT *JAMESON* SAID HE NEEDS AN *ASSOCIATE* AND I GOT *JUST* THE RIGHT *FRIENDS*.

SHUT UP, BLANDERS.

I'M NO LONER, GLORI...

YOU'RE CLOSE TO *LOSING* THAT *ARM*.

BEN URICH. DAILY BUGLE.

HEGERFORS.

COOGAN.

KLIK

klak KliK

URICH, LOIS...

DON'T HAVE TO *LOCK* IT, COOGAN. THERE'S *PLENTY* OF US...

COOGAN --WHAT ARE YOU--

WH--

217

WHMPP

YOUR *PREDECESSOR*--THE *FIRST* SUPER SOLDIER--FACED SIMPLER *TIMES* THAN OURS, MY FRIEND...AND SIMPLER *WARS*. SO MUCH HAS CHANGED.

SO MUCH...WE WHO *LOVE* AMERICA ARE NOW *SURROUNDED* --BY LYING *ASSASSINS* AND SOFT-HEARTED *FOOLS*.

WE *PATRIOTS*-- THEY *LAUGH* AT US, MY *SON*...

...I AM *SORRY*. YOU REMIND ME SO OF MY *OWN* SON--A *FINE* BOY HE IS, A *VETERAN*...

...I SHALL BE *HONEST* WITH YOU. THERE ARE *MANY* WHO *OPPOSE* ME.

I AM UNDER CONSTANT *SCR...* BY THE *POLICE*. I AM, IN TH... *STRICTEST* DEFINITION OF LAW, A *CRIMINAL*.

I KNOW T... *STARTLES* Y... BUT, AS I SAI... SO MUCH HAS CH... AMERICA'S *ENE...* HAVE GROWN SO S... THAT OUR *BOYS...* IN ASIAN *JUN...*

--AND C... *PEOPLE* W... NOT *HON...* THEM...

OUR *BOYS...*

...AND IT *TORTURES* ME THAT THE NOBLE CONCEPT OF *FREE ENTERPRISE*--THE CROWNING *TRIUMPH* OF OUR FOREFATHERS--HAS BEEN *MURDERED* BY ENDLESS, CORROSIVE *LEGISLATION.*

TO SIMPLY KEEP SOME *SHADOW* OF THAT DREAM *ALIVE,* I MUST... MUST *BREAK* THE LAW...

...EXCUSE ME...I...

STILL, WE ARE NOT *ALONE,* NUKE. THERE ARE *OTHERS* WHO BELIEVE--ENOUGH, BARELY ENOUGH OF US, TO KEEP THE *HOPE* ALIVE.

WE WHO...*DECIDE* SUCH THINGS HAVE FORMED A PROUD *TRINITY*--OF *STATE*--AND *MILITARY*--AND *BUSINESS.* WE MUST HAVE *UNITY*--AGAINST THE *MADNESS* THAT SURROUNDS US--AGAINST THE *INFECTION* OF THE AMERICAN *SPIRIT.*

THERE ARE THOSE WHO SAY THAT *UNITY* IS *CONSPIRACY*--THAT *AMERICA* IS *EVIL*--

I KNOW WHAT THEY SAY. I KNOW WHAT THEY SAY.

--AND NOW A SINGLE *MAN* THREATENS TO *DESTROY* WHAT WE HAVE BUILT. HE MOVES *AGAINST* ME--CALLS ME A *VILLAIN.*

I AM *NOT* A VILLAIN, MY SON. I AM A *CORPORA-TION*--IN THE *CONGLOMER-ATE* THAT IS *AMERICA.* BUT HIS ALLIES IN THE *PRESS*--

THE *PRESS...*

WHERE IS HE?

HELL'S KITCHEN.

221

HELL'S KITCHEN IS ACHING *MUSCLES* AND GROWLING *STOMACHS* -- CHILDREN'S FEET ON BROKEN *GLASS* -- HOPELESS *LAUGHTER,* ECHOING ACROSS AN EMPTY *LOT.*

HELL'S KITCHEN IS WHERE I WAS *BORN* -- AND BORN *AGAIN.*

THE BURGERS SIZZLE AND *SNAP.* THE BACON *POPS* ON THE GRIDDLE, NEARLY READY. THE *EGGS* -- THEY'RE THE *BEST* PART --

--OVER EASY-- HOT SECONDS TO GET THEM JUST *SOLID* ENOUGH-- THEN *FLIP THEM* -- NEATLY, QUICKLY--

--THEN GET THEM *OFF* WHILE THE YOLK IS STILL QUIVERING, BARELY CONTAINED...

...ANOTHER DAY *PASSES.* A NOTHER DAY OF *WAITING.*

QUITTING TIME, RED, SEE YOU IN THE *MORNING.*

GIVE THE *BURGERS* ABOUT TEN MORE *SECONDS* AND THEY'LL BE *PERFECT.*

GOOD *CROWD* TONIGHT--

--THAT *COUGH* --

--BEN...

...HE SOUNDS LIKE HE'S IN *SHOCK*...

...I COME HERE TO *WRITE.* FOOD'S *TERRIBLE* SO NOBODY'S EVER *HERE.*

LOOKS PRETTY *CROWDED* TO ME.

YOU LOOK *THIN,* RED. TAKE THIS *HOME.* YOU NEVER *HAD* SUCH *COBBLER.*

TERRIBLE NEIGHBORHOOD...

HELL'S KITCHEN. *RIGHT.* LOUSY NEIGHBORHOOD, *DANGEROUS.* BUT MATT WAS *BORN* HERE AND I--

--DID I-- DID I REALLY *KILL* THAT MAN --

YOU *SAVED* OUR *LIVES,* BEN.

BEST BURGER I EVER *HAD*...

CAN'T HELP YOU YET, BEN. CAN'T BE SEEN WITH *ANYONE*, UNTIL--

--THAT *SOUND*...

...CHECKED MATT'S *MEDICAL RECORDS* AND FOUND SOMETHING *FUNNY*. IT'S ABOUT HIS MOTHER --MATT ALWAYS SAID SHE *DIED* GIVING *BIRTH* TO HIM, BUT...

...*BLANDERS*. I REALLY *KILLED* HIM...

Diner

...THAT'S NO *POLICE* HELICOPTER...

THE *CLUE* WAS SLIM INDEED --THE WORDS OF A *THIRD-RATE THUG* WHO CLAIMS HE HAD THE PLEASURE OF STABBING MURDOCK SOME DAYS PAST.

IT WOULD BE A LOGICAL HIDING PLACE. IT HOLDS MANY OF THE *LOST* AND *NAMELESS*. IT WAS HIS *HOME*, AS A BOY.

YES. MURDOCK WILL *REVEAL HIMSELF*-- WHEN HELL'S KITCHEN BURNS.

SKIP THE *NAPALM*, BOY. THOSE ARE *AMERICANS*. JUST *MESS THINGS UP*. LITTLE *PROPERTY DAMAGE* CAN GO A LONG *WAY*.

WE'RE BRINGING YOU IN *LOW*...

LOW, TOO *NEAR* THE STREET--THE *MOTOR*, *ROARING*--

--*DUST* AND *DIRT* AND BLOWING *GARBAGE*--

--*COUGHING*--*STARTLED GASPS*--AN *ANGRY SHOUT*--

-- *SOMETHING HUMAN*--*HISSES*--

OUR *BOYS*--

BQAKA RAKABPSKKK

THREE-- NO-- IT'S FOUR BLOCKS AWAY--

--BULLETS CUT THROUGH FLESH AND BONE--

--A WOMAN HOLDS HER BABY CLOSE AND HEARS HIM GURGLE--

--A LUNG COLLAPSES--

--THREE BLOCKS NOW-- A MAN CHOKES OUT HALF A NAME AND DIES--

PFAMM

--FROM THE GUN-- A ROCKET--

WHOOM

--A WINO CRIES TO GOD--

GET YOUR CAMERA.

PFAMM

224

--ANOTHER ROCKET-- HEADED FOR--

--KAREN...

WHOOM

MOVING *UP*, BOY-- GOT *COMPANY*--

ONE MORE--

BRAMM

MATT-- AM I *DYING*?

NO, NO, HONEY.

EVERYTHING *IMPORTANT* IN YOU--IS *SAFE*.

SAFE. I KEPT *IT* SAFE FOR YOU, MATT.

I THOUGHT I'D HAVE TO BE A LOT MORE *PATIENT* THAN THIS, KINGPIN.

I THOUGHT I'D HAVE TO *WAIT* FOR *WEEKS*--

--FOR YOU TO GET *SLOPPY*-- LIKE YOU DID WITH MY *HOUSE*.

KOWEE KOWEEE KOWEE

ENEMY FIRE.

A CHOPPER.

PFAMM

THE PILOT SCREAMS AN ALERT--THE GUNNER GOES TO HIS DEATH WITH A CURSE--

--TWO LOVERS SLEEP QUIETLY--

--THE SCREAMING STARTS.

FROM EVERYWHERE.

HE PASSES CLOSE--

THWAKK

SPAKK

FARP

GIVE ME A RED.

226

NEXT: ARMAGEDDON

PART FIVE

TO SPAN THE SPACEWAYS

SAY, did you wonder why we didn't show you the cover of the magazine in which The Watcher's origin story appeared? That's because it's the very same magazine in which our next origin tale appears. Since we don't want to show you the same cover twice, I decided to save it till you finish reading this scintillating section, the very last intro I'll be writing for this valiant little volume.

And so we come to the big one, perhaps the most long-awaited origin tale of all. Let me clear my mind of earthbound matters as I return in memory once again to the early days of Marvel—to the beginning of The Silver Surfer.

The year is 1966. The scene is a little luncheonette where Jack Kirby and I had gone for a quick bite, and where we could continue our discussion of what to do for the next issue of *Fantastic Four*. The FF had already fought Dr. Doom, The Mole Man, The Sub-Mariner, and many, many other superpowerful foes. Both Jack and I were wracking our brains for some opponent who would be able to offer a still greater challenge than any of those the FF had yet encountered. We knew we needed a menace which would prove to be dynamic, daring, and totally different. Sounds easy, huh?

There's no need to make you suffer through the whole tortuous process with us. Suffice it to say that we eventually came up with just what we had been looking for. The FF's next super-foe would be more than just a man, more than just a group of men, more than a mere creature from another planet, or any group of planets. No, the FF's next super-foe would be a seemingly omnipotent being who could destroy entire planets at will . . . who could alter and reshape entire worlds . . . who was as superior to Homo sapiens as a man is to an ant. The FF's next super-foe would be—Galactus!

It's hard to describe Galactus' impact upon our readers without having you think I'm exaggerating. The fans went ape. Our sales soared. The fan mail nearly smothered us. In a word, Galactus was a smash.

Actually, the Galactus tale was stretched over three consecutive issues. Which reminds me—one of the biggest kicks I get, when speaking at a college, is during the questions-and-answers part of my little performance. Inevitably, someone will shout out a question about "The Galactus Trilogy." Yes, "The Galactus Trilogy"—that's the way I've heard it referred to on campuses from Maine to New Mexico—and it really knocks me out. It has the same prestigious sound to it as "The Harvard Classics," or "The Dead Sea Scrolls." But, in case you're wondering what all this tintinnabulating trivia has to do with The Silver Surfer ...

After we had discussed the plot for (are you ready for this?) "The Galactus Trilogy," Jack spent the next few weeks drawing the first 20-page installment. When he brought it to me so that I could add the dialogue and captions, I was surprised to find a brand-new character floating around the artwork—a silver-skinned, smooth-domed, sky-riding surfer atop a speedy flying surfboard. When I asked ol' Jackson who he was, Jack replied something to the effect that a supremely powerful gent like Galactus, a godlike giant who roamed the galaxies, would surely require the services of a herald who could serve him as an advance guard.

I liked the idea. More than that, I was wild about the new character. It didn't take long for us to christen him with the only logical appellation for a silver-skinned surfboarder—namely, The Silver Surfer.

Later, as I started to write the dialogue for the strip, I realized that The Surfer had the potential to be far more than just a high-flying, colorful supporting character. Studying the illustrations, seeing the way Jack had drawn him, I found a certain nobility in his demeanor, an almost spiritual quality in his aspect and his bearing. In determining what his speech pattern would be, I began to imagine the way that a space-born apostle would speak. There seemed something biblically pure about our Silver Surfer, something totally selfless and magnificently innocent. As you can gather, I was tempted to imbue him with a spirit of almost religious purity. In short, the more I studied him, the more I got into his thoughts and his dialogue, the more I saw him as someone who would graphically represent all the best, the most unselfish, qualities of intelligent life. It was a tall order,

I'll admit, but that's what makes the comicbook world so exciting.

After completing our trilogy, we were besieged and bombarded by impassioned requests to give The Silver Surfer his own magazine. I would have cheerfully complied, except for one thing. Jack was too busy drawing The Fantastic Four, The Avengers, Thor, The X-Men, Sgt. Fury And His You-Know-Whats, and countless other features and covers as well; while I was writing 'most everything Jack was illustrating, plus a number of other features. Neither of us had time to take an extra breath, let alone tackle a new and highly important magazine. Most of our other top artists and writers were likewise working to full capacity, and The Silver Surfer just wasn't the kind of character you'd easily hand over to any joker who could hold a pencil. And so he stayed out of circulation, except for a guest appearance here and there, till August 1968—the time that things really began to break loose.

By '68 we were cheerfully expanding in a million directions at once. It seemed that every time we turned around we'd find a new artist or two, some new writers or editorial assistants, and of course some new superhero magazines. By this time, I'd been lucky enough to hire Roy Thomas as my editorial assistant, and it wasn't long before the rascally one had taken enough of the scripting chores off my weary, sagging shoulders so that I could find the time to write a new Silver Surfer series. The only problem was—where would I find the one to draw it? And now, since you've asked . . .

Marvel Comics must have been born under some sort of lucky star. Whenever we need anything desperately, it always seems to fall into our collective lap. Thus, at that time, I had received one of the most fateful phone calls of my career. It was a voice from the past—the voice of John Buscema!

Big John Buscema had been one of Marvel's youngest and most capable artists for a short period of time in the 1950's. Then, for some reason or other, he developed a case of wanderlust and journeyed off to seek fame and fortune in the field of advertising illustration. I hadn't heard from him or seen him in years. And now, suddenly, there he was on the phone, telling me he was sick and tired of doing illustrations of cola bottles and automobiles for advertisements—he wanted to come back, back to Marvel, back where the action was.

I didn't answer him immediately. I was too busy doing cartwheels. Finally, when I caught my breath, I shouted, "What are you waiting for? Get right over here. We'll have a brand-new pencil waiting for you—hang the expense!" And so, a new era opened up for mighty Marvel—or perhaps I should say for mighty lucky Marvel—John Buscema had come home again.

The months passed and Big John made his mark on many strips—The Fantastic Four, Spider-Man, The Avengers—how's that for starters? But then I asked him the big question—would he want to do a new Silver Surfer series? Ol' Johnny, who's about as temperamental as this typewriter I'm pounding on, yawned and said, "I guess so," which was about the biggest emotional outburst he'd made all year. Of such gossamer things are legends created.

I was so excited about the prospect of a Silver Surfer magazine that I convinced the moneybags behind Marvel to make it a bigger book than the average title. And so, while most of the other comics were 32 pages and sold for 12¢, we made *The Silver Surfer* a 25-center, and jam packed it with 64 pages of sheer Marvel magic.

The story you are about to rapturously read is the first in the series. In this tale we devoted a full 38-page novel-length saga to the origin of The Surfer. You'll travel to legendary Zenn-La, you'll meet the stunning Shalla Bal, you'll encounter The Hulk, Dr. Doom, The Fantastic Four, and Galactus himself. You'll see the destruction of a world and the re-creation of a being. You'll see some of the finest artwork ever to grace a comicbook's pages. Of course, in order to know what's going on, you'll also have to read my story—but then, you can't have everything.

And now the time is come. Once again I usher you into the sparkling world of Marvel, where you dare encounter fantasy and fable to fill your soul with wonder. If you will be reading "The Origin of The Silver Surfer" for the first time, I envy your thrill of discovery. If, like me, you've read it before, I hope you'll enjoy it anew, like savoring the mellow glow of an old friendship rekindled. Either way, don't waste another second on this page. The cosmos lies before us—and the spaceways beckon!

SENTINEL OF THE SPACEWAYS!

THE SILVER SURFER

MARVEL COMICS GROUP

25¢ IND.   1 AUG

BIG PREMIERE ISSUE

THE ORIGIN OF THE SILVER SURFER!

AN ALL-NEW BOOK-LENGTH MARVEL EPIC!

THE MOST EAGERLY-AWAITED EPIC OF THE YEAR!

The ORIGIN OF THE SILVER SURFER!

ONE OF COMICDOM'S GREATEST COLLABORATIONS!

PROUDLY PRESENTED BY STAN (THE MAN) LEE and JOHN (BLOOD'N GUTS) BUSCEMA

EMBELLISHMENT: JOE SINNOTT

LETTERING: SAM ROSEN

HIGH OER THE ROOF OF THE WORLD HE SOARS... FREE AND UNFETTERED AS THE ROARING WIND ITSELF! BEHOLD THE SKY-BORN SPANNER OF A TRILLION GALAXIES... THE RESTLESS, STREAKING STRANGER FROM THE FARTHEST REACH OF SPACE... THIS GLISTENING, GLEAMING SEEKER OF TRUTH, WHOM MAN SHALL CALL FOREVERMORE--

The SILVER SURFER!

SUDDENLY, UNEXPECTEDLY, BEFORE THE PIERCING, PENETRATING EYES OF THE SPEEDING SURFER, A BLAZING, OUT-OF-CONTROL *CAPSULE* HURTLES DOWN FROM ORBIT...

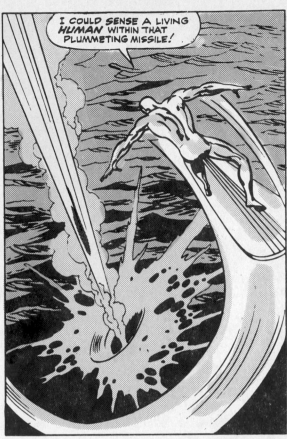

I COULD SENSE A LIVING *HUMAN* WITHIN THAT PLUMMETING MISSILE!

...A HUMAN WHO IS IN MOST GRAVE *DANGER*...

FOR, HE DOES NOT *STIR* WITHIN HIS SUNKEN METAL SHELL... AND HIS LIFE-GIVING SUPPLY OF OXYGEN WILL SOON BE *GONE!*

I CANNOT PERMIT A FELLOW BEING... TO *PERISH*... WHILE IT IS WITHIN MY POWER TO *SAVE* HIM!

TO ONE WHO HAS ENDURED THE AIRLESS VACUUMS OF THE UNENDING *COSMOS*...

IT MATTERS *NOT* WHETHER I SPAN THE EMPTINESS OF *SPACE*, OR THE WATERY VASTNESS OF THE UNDERSEA *DEEPS!*

2.

A SIMPLE THRUST OF CONCENTRATED *COSMIC FORCE* WILL BE SUFFICIENT TO *OPEN* THE HATCH I SEE BEFORE ME!

FORTUNATELY HE STILL WEARS HIS PROTECTIVE HELMET!

IT WILL *PROTECT* HIM UNTIL WE SEEK THE SAN OF THE *SKY*

THEN, SECONDS LATER...

AIRCRAFT... SEARCHING... PROBING THE AREA!

THEY ARE SEEKING *HIM* WHOM I HAVE *FOUND!*

3.

BLUE LEADER TO BATBOY BRIGADE! WE'VE *FOUND* OUR MISSING *MUDHAWK!*

VEERING SHARPLY AT *ELEVEN O'CLOCK!*

HE'S BEEN *CAPTURED*... SINGLE-HANDED... BY *SILVER SURFER!*

CONTACT FLOATING *DEN MOTHER!* THEY'RE HEADING RIGHT *TOWARDS* HER!

236

CIRCLE him! FORCE him DOWN!

IT IS BEYOND BELIEF! THEY actually ATTACK me!

HE'S EVADING us! LET 'IM HAVE IT!

IN EVERY PART OF THE GLOBE IT IS THE SAME! HATRED, FEAR AND UNREASONING HOSTILITY HAVE POSSESSED MEN'S HEARTS!

BUT, THE SILVER SURFER WILL HAVE NO PART OF IT!

DID YOU SEE THAT?

HE INCREASED HIS SPEED...AND ZOOMED OVER THE HORIZON LIKE A METEOR!

HE MUST BE HALF-WAY AROUND THE WORLD BY NOW!

BLUE LEADER TO MUDHAWKS ---RETURN TO ROOST!

...OUR PIGEON'S FLOWN THE COOP!

WITHIN SECONDS, ALMOST EVERY CAPITAL ON EARTH IS VISITED BY THE SILVERY, STREAKING SURFBOARD AND ITS SKY-BORN MASTER...

BUT, COMMISSAR... HE HAS PENETRATED OUR MISSILE DEFENSES AS THOUGH THEY DO NOT EXIST!

WE MUST ACT! WE MUST DO SOMETHING!

OF COURSE, GENERAL ...OF COURSE!

WE WILL REMAIN CALM ---AND TOTALLY IGNORE THE ENTIRE INCIDENT!

HE IS HEADING TOWARDS PEIPING!

WE SHALL ALLOW OUR ACCURSED ORIENTAL COMRADES TO DEAL WITH HIM!

BUT, THE TOTAL POWER OF THE RED CHINESE IS EQUALLY INEFFECTUAL AGAINST THE SPEEDING SURFER...

I COULD DESTROY THEM WITH A SINGLE COSMIC BLAST! BUT, TO WHAT AVAIL?

IT IS AN IMPERIALIST PLOT AGAINST THE SECURITY OF THE PEOPLES' REPUBLIC!

WE MUST PRINT A MILLION NEW POSTERS...

CALL OUT THE RED GUARD!

WITH THE SUBLIME THOUGHTS OF CHAIRMAN MAO!

5.

BUT, NEITHER *MISSILES* NOR MEANINGLESS *MOUTHINGS* OF PETTY PEDAGOGUES CAN HALT THE PROGRESS OF THE *SILVER SURFER,* NOR STIFLE THE *LONGING* IN HIS TORTURED *SOUL...*

IN ALL THE *GALAXIES...* IN ALL THE ENDLESS REACHES OF *SPACE...*

I HAVE FOUND *NO PLANET* MORE BLESSED THAN *THIS...*

NO WORLD MORE LAVISHLY ENDOWED WITH NATURAL *BEAUTY* ...WITH GENTLE *CLIMATE*... WITH EVERY INGREDIENT TO CREATE A VIRTUAL LIVING *PARADISE!*

POSSESSED OF *RAINFALL* IN GREAT ABUNDANCE... *SOIL* FERTILE ENOUGH TO FEED A *GALAXY!*

AND A *SUN---* EVER-WARM--- EVER CONSTANT--- EVER SYMBOLIZING NEW LIFE, NEW *HOPE!*

IT IS AS THOUGH THE *HUMAN RACE* HAS BEEN DIVINELY *FAVORED* OVER ALL WHO LIVE!

AND *YET...* IN THEIR UNCONTROLLABLE *INSANITY...* IN THEIR UNFORGIVABLE *BLINDNESS...* THEY SEEK TO *DESTROY* THIS SHINING JEWEL... THIS SOFTLY-SPINNING *GEM...*

...THIS TINY *BLESSED SPHERE...* WHICH MEN CALL *EARTH!*

WHILE, *TRAPPED* UPON THIS WORLD OF MAD-NESS... STAND *I!*

HOW MUCH *LONGER* AM I DESTINED TO ENDURE A FATE I CANNOT EVEN *COMPREHEND!*

HOW MUCH *LONGER* BEFORE MY EYES MAY ONCE AGAIN BEHOLD THE WONDERS OF THE EVER-CHANGING *COSMOS*...

HOW MUCH *LONGER* BEFORE MY EXILE *ENDS*... AND I MAY STAND ONCE MORE UPON THE LAND THAT GAVE ME *BIRTH*??

EVEN *NOW*, I CAN RECALL THOSE EARLY DAYS...THOSE YOUTHFUL YEARS... UPON THE PLANET *ZENN-LA*!

"HOW WELL I REMEMBER THE YEARNING...THE QUESTIONING... THE ACHING *DISCONTENT* WHICH FILLED MY HEART...EVEN *THEN*..."

OUR RACE HAS ACHIEVED THE *PERFECTION* THAT ALL OTHERS DREAM OF!

WAR... CRIME... ILLNESS... THEY ARE BUT DIMLY-REMEMBERED MEMORIES!

WE HAVE ACHIEVED *ALL!* NO GOALS REMAIN!

AND YET, MAN WAS MEANT TO *STRIVE*...TO *STRUGGLE*... TO *YEARN!*

THOSE TO WHOM NO DISTANT *HORIZONS* BECKON---FOR WHOM NO *CHALLENGES* REMAIN ---

THOUGH THEY HAVE INHERITED A *UNIVERSE*... THEY POSSESS ONLY EMPTY *SAND!*

BUT I WILL NOT SUFFER SUCH A FATE!

I WILL NOT SPEND A LIFE-TIME IN *IDLE-NESS*...IN THE SHALLOW PUR-SUIT OF ENDLESS *PLEASURE!*

THOUGH WE HAVE ACHIEVED *NIRVANA*...

IT WAS *GAINED* FOR US BY THOSE WHO CAME *BEFORE!*

WE HAVE NOT *EARNED* IT!

THEREFORE! IT IS NOT TRULY *OURS!*

THIS IS IT... THE ULTIMATE *BEGINNING*...

EXACTLY AS IT BEGAN ON SO MANY PLANETS.... IN SO MANY COUNTLESS WORLDS!

...ONLY TO BE FOLLOWED, EONS LATER, BY THE TEN-THOUSAND CENTURY *AGE OF WARFARE*...

WHICH LEFT *BATTLE SCARS* SO DEEP, THAT WE *RE-NOUNCED* THE USE OF ARMS...*FOREVER!*

AND, THEN AT LAST... THE *GOLDEN AGE OF REASON!*

THE HUNDRED CENTURIES WHICH BROUGHT LEARNING, AND WISDOM, AND *PEACE* TO OUR WAR-RAVAGED GALAXY!

9.

MORE! I MUST SEE *MORE!*

ONLY BY STUDYING THE *PAST* WILL I LEARN WHY THE *PRESENT* IS...TO *ME*...SO TOTALLY *UNENDURABLE!*

ATTENDANT!

I DESIRE TO STUDY THE EARLY DAYS OF ZENN-LA *SPACE TRAVEL!*

INSTANTANEOUSLY, THE MUSEUM'S *MENTAL TRANSPORTATION ELEMENT* GIVES THE EAGER *NORRIN RADD* A TOTAL SENSATION OF ACTUALLY BEING *PRESENT* AT THE LAUNCHING OF ONE OF ZENN-LA'S MIGHTY *STAR SHIPS,* AGES AGO DURING THE LONG-EXTINCT DAYS OF THE PLANET'S EARLY SPACE PROGRAM...

THIS WAS THE TIME OF MY PEOPLE'S GREATEST GLORY...

THE TIME WE DARED TO *REACH* FOR THE DISTANT STARS AND GALAXIES!

AN ENTIRE *UNIVERSE* WAS BECKONING TO US...

AND WE HAD THE *COURAGE*... WE HAD THE *WILL*... TO PROBE THE VAST-NESS OF THE DISTANT *UNKNOWN!*

OUR GREATEST HEROES WERE THE FEARLESS, SPACE-SPANNING *ASTRONAUTS*...

---THE TIME-HONORED *ASTRO-PIONEERS* TO WHOM *NO* JOURNEY WAS TOO FAR... *NO* WORLD WAS TOO FORBIDDING!

BUT THEN, ONE DAY... IT *ENDED!*

WE HAD PROBED THE COSMOS... SET OUR FLAG UPON A THOUSAND GALAXIES!

WE HAD GONE TOO FAR... SEEN TOO MUCH! AND THEN... WE NO LONGER CARED!

WE OF ZENN LA... WHO HAD SCATTERED OUR SEED TO THE MOST DISTANT STARS...

RETURNED TO OUR MOTHER WORLD... NEVER TO VENTURE FORTH AGAIN!

FOR US, THE AGE OF SPACE TRAVEL HAD DIED...

NEVER TO BE BORN AGAIN!

CLOSING TIME, CITIZEN! THE SESSION IS ENDED!

ALL IS ENDED! NOTHING REMAINS... SAVE STARK AND BLEAK DECAY!

AND NOW I STAND UPON ANOTHER WORLD... FAR YOUNGER... FAR MORE PRIMITIVE...

A WORLD AT THE CROSS-ROADS!

AND NO MAN MAY PREDICT WHICH PATH IT WILL ELECT TO FOLLOW!

BUT WAIT! I HEAR THE SOUND OF MUFFLED FOOTPADS APPROACHING!

11.

YETIS! THE WILD, SAVAGE SNOW-DWELLERS...

THE SO-CALLED ABOMINABLE SNOWMEN OF EARTHLY LEGEND!

THEY THINK ME AN ENEMY! THEY RUSH TO ATTACK... WITHOUT QUESTION OR PAUSE!

EVEN *THEY*... POOR, UNTHINKING CREATURES OF THE FROZEN WASTES...

...HAVE BEEN SO *HOUNDED*...SO *RUTHLESSLY HUNTED* FOR TIME WITHOUT MEASURE...

THAT THEY FEAR *ANY* WHO INVADE THEIR DESOLATE DOMAIN!

AND, LIKE SO *MANY* WHO ATTACK *WITHOUT* REASON...

HOW OFTEN IS BLIND, UNREASONING *FEAR* THE CAUSE... RATHER THAN NAKED *SAVAGERY*?

THEY SEEK TO *SMASH* ME TO THE GROUND... TO FELL MY BY SHEER WEIGHT OF NUMBERS!

AND I HAVE NOT THE *WORDS* TO TURN ASIDE THEIR *WRATH!*

SINCE I DO NOT WISH TO *HARM* THEM, I SHALL TRY *ANOTHER* MEANS...!

LET MY *SURFBOARD* FLOAT... AND THUS ATTRACT THEIR BESTIAL *ATTENTION!*

SECONDS LATER...TWO HUGE, CLUTCHING *HANDS* SEIZE THE STRANGELY ALIEN OBJECT...

IT IS *DONE!* THEY HAVE *FORGOTTEN* ME!

NOW, AS THEY *BATTLE* FOR THEIR PRIZE... LIKE THE BRUTES THEY ARE...

LET MY *BOARD* AND ME AGAIN BECOME AS *ONE!*

FOR I MUST *LEAVE* THIS PLACE OF *MADNESS!*

12

AND YET, WHERE CAN I GO?

THE CELESTIAL CURRENTS OF SPACE ARE FOREVERMORE *DENIED* ME!

AND, ON ALL OF *EARTH*, THERE IS NO HAVEN...NO SHELTER FOR THE LIKES OF *ME!*

EACH AND EVERY EARTHLING, IN HIS OWN TRAGIC WAY, IS AS MUCH A *YETI* AS THOSE WHO FIGHT BELOW!

ONLY THE OUTWARD *TRAPPINGS* DIFFER...BUT ALL THEIR HEARTS ARE FILLED WITH *FEAR...* AND DARK *DISTRUST!*

EVEN THOSE I HAVE *BEFRIENDED* ...HAVE TURNED *AGAINST* ME!

ONE THERE WAS... MEN CALLED HIM *HULK*...A DAZED AND TORTURED TITAN FOR WHOM I FELT DEEP *KINSHIP...!* *

LOOK! THAT GUY ON A FLYING *SURFBOARD!!* HE'S HELPING THE HULK *ESCAPE!*

AS DRAMATICALLY DEPICTED IN *TALES TO ASTONISH* # *93!*...SEMI-CLASSICAL STAN.

13

"THOUGH *OTHERS* CALLED HIM MONSTER, TO *ME* HE WAS A FELLOW BEING...IN NEED OF AID!"

"I WISHED ONLY TO BRING HIM TO A PLACE OF *SAFETY!* I WISHED ONLY TO CALL HIM *FRIEND!*"

"BUT, ONCE AGAIN, I *FAILED!* HE, WHO HAD BEEN SO TORMENTED, NOW *TURNED*...THRU A FATEFUL MISUNDERSTANDING...UPON HIS BENEFACTOR..!"

STAY BACK! I MEAN YOU NO HARM!

NOBODY HARMS THE *HULK!*

"SADLY, I REALIZED HE WOULD NOT HEED AN APPEAL TO *REASON*.."

THERE IS ONLY *ONE* COURSE OPEN TO ME...

I AM FORCED TO RESORT TO ...A MILD *COSMIC BOLT!*

"THERE WERE *OTHERS*... MANY OTHERS! NEVER SHALL I FORGET THE ONE CALLED... *DOCTOR DOOM*...""

"*UNSUSPECTINGLY,* I APPROACHED HIS *LONELY CASTLE*..."

*AS WE RABID READERS OF *FANTASTIC FOUR #57* SHALL NE'ER FORGET! ---SOULFUL STAN.

HE MADE ME *WELCOME* WITHIN THE COLD, GREY WALLS THAT HOUSED HIS COURT! I TOLD HIM FROM WHENCE I HAD COME...AS HE LISTENED IN STONY SILENCE!

THOUGH MY *POWER* BEGGARS MERE DESCRIPTION...

STILL AM I A *PRISONER* UPON THIS SAVAGE WORLD!

HOW COULD I HAVE KNOWN THAT THE BROODING MONARCH IN WHOM I PLACED MY *TRUST* HAD BUT *ONE* SINISTER OBJECTIVE...

AND, EVEN AS I GAZED UPON THE DISTANT, BECKONING STARS...

...HE *STRUCK*...WITHOUT MERCY... WITHOUT HESITATION...*STRIPPING* ME OF MY COSMIC, SKY-SPAWNED *POWERS*...!

EVEN AS I FELL TO THE DANK STONE FLOOR...EVEN AS *DOCTOR DOOM* VOWED TO CONQUER ALL MANKIND WITH THE POWER HE HAD STOLEN FROM ME...I VOWED *NEVER AGAIN* TO TRUST ANOTHER HUMAN!

I KNEW AT LAST... THERE WAS NO REFUGE ON EARTH... FOR THE *SILVER SURFER!*

BUT, I PERSEVERED... AND, IN THE END, IT WAS THE ARMORED *ARCH-FIEND* WHO TASTED GRIM *DEFEAT!*

SO *NOW,* I RIDE THE ETERNAL *WINDS* ONCE MORE!

AND *NONE* SHALL EVER BE... MY *MASTER!*

BUT WHAT IS *THAT...* HALF HIDDEN IN THE FROZEN WASTES *BELOW...?*

AN ANCIENT *ENTRANCE...* BLOCKED BY THE THOUSAND-YEAR *WEIGHT* OF AN EVER-CRUMBLING HILLSIDE!

BUT, AN ENTRANCE TO... *WHAT??*

A MONSTROUS *CAVERN...* WHICH HAS NOT FELT THE TREAD OF HUMAN FEET SINCE TIME IMMEMORIAL!

AND YET... WHAT IS *THAT...* AHEAD OF ME?

NO SIMPLE, NATURAL CAVE IS *THIS!*

WHAT FANTASTIC *RELIC* OF A BYGONE AGE HAVE I STUMBLED ONTO?

16

I SEEM TO HEAR HER VOICE... GENTLE AS THE MIST AT DAWNING... ON THAT TRAGIC, FATEFUL DAY...

YOUR HEART IS STILL *TROUBLED* NORRIN RADD!

IT IS *NOTHING,* SHALLA!

MERELY A *MOOD* THAT SOON SHALL PASS!

I AM NOT DECEIVED, MY LOVE!

TOO LONG HAVE I SENSED THE *HUNGER* GNAWING AT YOUR BREAST!

...A HUNGER FOR THAT WHICH *I* CAN NEVER GIVE YOU!

THAT WHICH YOU DO CRAVE CAN BE *NO-WHERE* FOUND--- LEST YOU JOURNEY BEYOND THE FARTHEST *STAR!*

BUT *WHAT* CAN IT BE THAT YOU SEEK? THERE IS *NO TREASURE* IN ALL THE UNIVERSE WHICH CANNOT BE FOUND *HERE*... IN AGELESS *ZENN-LA!*

LOOK *ABOUT* YOU, NORRIN RADD... SEE THE *WONDERS* OF THIS WORLD OF WORLDS... SEE THE *GLORIES* WHICH ARE OURS... MERELY FOR THE *TAKING!*

NO, SHALLA... *NO!* THAT WHICH IS MINE FOR THE TAKING IS NOT *WORTH* THE TAKING!

PARADISE UNEARNED IS BUT A LAND OF *SHADOWS!*

I CAN NO LONGER BEAR THE *SIGHT* OF MY FELLOW MAN... SPENDING HIS DAYS IN PURSUIT OF END-LESS *PLEASURE*..!

EVEN OUR *KNOWLEDGE* IS UNEARNED! A LIFE-TIME'S LEARNING IS ABSORBED IN *MINUTES* BY OUR HYPNO-POWERED *STUDY-CUBES!*

AND WE NEED WANT FOR *NOTHING*...SO LONG AS WE CAN CREATE *ANY SUBSTANCE* VIA AN INEXPENSIVE *CYBERNO-MATERIALIZER!*

BUT, MOCKERY OF *ALL* MOCKERIES IS OUR *PARLIAMENT!*

HOUR AFTER HOUR, THE MOST LEARNED OF ALL STATESMEN *DEBATE* WITH GREAT SOLEMNITY...

THOUGH THEIR *BABBLE* IS *MEANINGLESS*... SINCE WE ARE GOVERNED BY *COMPUTERS!*

BUT, MINE IS A LOST AND LONELY VOICE... AND THERE ARE *NONE* TO LISTEN!

19

252

"IT WAS AT THAT VERY MOMENT...A MOMENT DESTINED TO CHANGE THE COURSE OF A BILLION BILLION LIVES...THAT THE FATEFUL *INTERRUPTION* OCCURRED..."

CAN YOU *NEVER* BE CONTENT? MUST YOU ALWAYS... *NORRIN*!!

BE *SILENT*, SHALLA!

THE *CITIZENS' ALARM* HAS SOUNDED...FOR THE FIRST TIME IN A *MILLENIUM*!

FREE MEN OF ZENN-LA... ATTEND YOU MY WORDS!

A GIGANTIC *ALIEN SPACE-CRAFT* HAS ENTERED OUR GALAXY, PIERCING ALL NUCLEAR *DEFENSES* AS THOUGH THEY ARE *NON-EXISTENT*

ALL CITIZENS MUST BE *PREPARED*...FOR A POSSIBLE *INVASION*!

NO! IT CANNOT *BE!*

WE HAVE NO *SPACE FLEET*.. NO *WEAPONS*!

WE'VE BEEN AT *PEACE* FOR AGES! WE'VE FORGOTTEN *HOW* TO FIGHT!

A WELL-TRAINED *ENEMY* CAN DESTROY US *ALL*!

NEVER! WE MAY BE UNPREPARED... BUT, IF WE ARE A PEOPLE *UNITED*.. WE *CANNOT* BE CONQUERED!

PERHAPS THE TASTE OF *DANGER* IS WHAT WE *NEED*...

TO MAKE US THE *MEN* OUR FOREFATHERS WERE!

20

253

AND, EVEN AS THE STARTLED CITIZENRY OF ZENN-LA OBSERVED THE FEARSOME, FATEFUL SPEEDING GLOBE...

SOMEHOW, I SENSE MY MOMENT OF DESTINY!

I SEEM TO FEEL THAT THE FATE OF NORRIN RADD IS INEXORABLY LINKED WITH THE UNKNOWN INVADER FROM SPACE!

WITHIN SECONDS, PANIC FILLED THE STREETS AS THE GIGANTIC, PLANET-GIRDLING GLOBE SPUN CLOSER...AND CLOSER...!

THERE IS NO PLACE TO FLEE!

IT WILL DESTROY US ALL!

ONLY OUR COMPUTERS CAN PROVIDE THE ANSWER!

THEY HAVE BEEN FED THE DATA...

WHAT SAY THEY NOW?

NEVER HAVE WE BEEN FACED WITH SUCH SEEMINGLY LIMITLESS POWER!

EVEN OUR INFALLIBLE COMPUTERS CAN GIVE US NO HOPE...NO CERTAIN DEFENSE!

BUT THEN, AS THE MYSTERIOUS, RAPIDLY-DESCENDING *SHIP*, SEEMED TO BLOT OUT THE VERY HEAVENS THEMSELVES...

THE *COMPUTERS* HAVE FINALLY RENDERED A *DECISION*...!

AGAINST SUCH *POWER ABSOLUTE*.. WE CAN EMPLOY NOTHING... SAVE THE *WEAPON SUPREME!*

THE *WEAPON*, *SUPREME!* IT IS ALMOST *UNTHINKABLE!*

NEVER BEFORE HAS IT BEEN EMPLOYED..

FOR, ITS *COBALT ENERGY* IS SO *DESTRUCTIVE*.. THAT EVEN *WE* MAY SUFFER FROM ITS EFFECT!

AND YET, WE HAVE *NO CHOICE!*

THE COMPUTER *MUST* BE OBEYED!

EMPLOY THE WEAPON SUPREME!

THEN, AT THE PRESS OF A BUTTON... THE DEED WAS *DONE*...!

NONE WHO *LIVED* DURING THAT MOMENTOUS DAY CAN EVER *FORGET* WHAT NEXT ENSUED...!

IT WAS LIKE A *UNIVERSE IN CHAOS*, AS NEIGHBORING PLANETOIDS *THEMSELVES* WERE INSTANTLY HURLED FROM *ORBIT*...!

BUT, MOMENTS AFTER THE DEBACLE...

HAVE I BEEN ASLEEP, NORRIN RADD?

NOT SO, SHALLA BAL!

AM I MERELY AWAKENING FROM A SAVAGE, INCOMPREHENSIBLE NIGHTMARE?

OUR WORST FEARS HAVE BEEN REALIZED! ZENN-LA TOTTERS ON THE BRINK OF DESTRUCTION!

YOU WERE BUT STUNNED BY THE FALLING DEBRIS!

HOW COULD IT HAVE HAPPENED?

BRIEF MOMENTS AGO WE WANTED FOR NOTHING! OUR WORLD WAS SECURE! BUT, NOW--!!

ALL WE CAN DO IS HELPLESSLY AWAIT... OUR FINAL SECONDS!

NO!

WE STILL HAVE OUR LIVES... OUR UN-CONQUERABLE SPIRIT!

WE MUST FIGHT.. AS OUR ANCESTOR WOULD HAVE DONE

WAIT! NO ONE CAN FIGHT THE IMPOSSIBLE!

NOTHING IS IMPOSSIBLE... EXCEPT TO ONE WHO HAS LOST THE WILL!

AND NORRIN RADD SHALL NEVER LOSE HIS WILL!

FOR WE MUST NOW BE TRUE TO THE PROUD HERITAGE OF ZENN-LA!

I MUST FIND THOSE WHO WILL JOIN ME...THOSE WHO WILL CLOSE RANKS TO MAKE A FINAL STAND!

BUT, THERE WERE *NONE* TO BE FOUND! NONE, SAVE THE INJURED, AND THE AILING, AND THE WEAK, AND THE TIMID!

LIKE ONE BEREFT OF *REASON* I COMBED THE SHATTERED STREETS ...DESPERATELY SEEKING AN *ALLY*---A *WEAPON*---ANY-*THING* WITH WHICH TO *FIGHT BACK!*

THE GLOBE COMES EVER *CLOSER!*

AND THERE ARE *NONE* TO GIVE IT PAUSE!

HELP ME! *HELP ME..* PLEASE..!

I *KNOW* YOU! YOU ARE ONE OF THE COUNCIL OF *SCIENTISTS!*

WHAT DOES THAT MATTER *NOW?*

WHAT DOES *ANYTHING* MATTER NOW..?

THERE IS NOTHING *LEFT* FOR US...SAVE *DEATH!*

BUT, WE KNOW *NOT* WHO ATTACKS US... NOR FOR WHAT *MOTIVE!*

IF I COULD BUT *REACH* THE GIANT GLOBE...IF I HAD A *SPACECRAFT* TO CARRY ME *ALOFT!*

BUT OUR FINEST *SCIENTIFIC MINDS* --- OUR GREATEST *COMPUTERS*--- HAVE ALL AGREED...

OUR PLIGHT IS *HOPELESS..* DO YOU HEAR? *HOPELESS?*

ONLY TO ONE WHO HAS *ABANDONED* FAITH!

SINCE ALL ARE AGREED...THERE IS *NO HOPE...* THEN SURELY WE HAVE NAUGHT TO *LOSE!*

THEREFORE, I *ASK* YOU....*BUILD* ME A SPACE SHIP....FOR I WOULD SEEK THE *INVADER!*

ALONE... AND *UNAIDED*...YOU WOULD DARE APPROACH ---THE *GLOBE?*

I *WOULD!*

THEN... YOU SHALL *HAVE* YOUR SHIP!

26.

QUICKLY SUMMONING OTHERS, THE AGED, LEARNED ONE SOON GATHERED THE NECESSARY MATERIAL...

YOU HAVE SERVED ME WELL!

NOW STAND ASIDE!—

IT IS I ALONE WHO MUST COMPLETE THE TASK!

TURN YOUR HEAD AWAY, NORRIN RADD...LEST THE ENERGY OF THIS MENTAL-CONSTRUCTOR CAUSE YOU INJURY!

WITHIN SECONDS, THE IMAGE OF YOUR SHIP WHICH I HAVE IN MY MIND...

--SHALL TAKE SOLID FORM BEFORE OUR EYES!

IT IS DONE!

YOU HAVE YOUR SPACE-CRAFT... COMPLETELY FUELED!

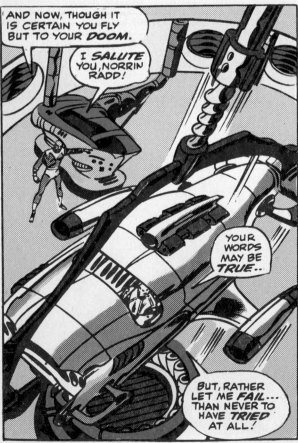

AND NOW, THOUGH IT IS CERTAIN YOU FLY BUT TO YOUR DOOM.

I SALUTE YOU, NORRIN RADD!

YOUR WORDS MAY BE TRUE...

BUT, RATHER LET ME FAIL... THAN NEVER TO HAVE TRIED AT ALL!

AGES AGO... A THOUSAND TIMES A THOUSAND WOULD HAVE BEGGED TO FLY THAT SHIP!

BUT NOW.. THERE IS ONLY... NORRIN RADD!

THE VESSEL I APPROACH IS FAR *LARGER* THAN I COULD HAVE DREAMED!

NOW...I MUST ATTEMPT...TO ESTABLISH *CONTACT!*

UNKNOWN STRANGER-- HEED THE WORDS OF *NORRIN RADD!*

I SPEAK FOR *ZENN-LA!* YOU MUST COME *NO CLOSER*... UNLESS YOU COME *IN PEACE!*

I WAS MET WITH *SILENCE!* A SILENCE SO *THICK*...SO *HEAVY* ...IT SEEMED TO COVER THE HEAVENS LIKE A *SHROUD!*

BUT THEN, SUDDENLY... UNEXPECT- EDLY...

SOMETHING *DRAWS* ME WITHIN THE GLOBE...

A POWER SO *GREAT*, RESISTANCE IS ALL BUT *UNTHINKABLE!*

THEN, WHEN I LEFT MY OWN TINY CRAFT...

THERE IS *NO CREW*... NO SIGN OF AN INVADING *ARMY!*

BUT SOMETHING DRAWS ME TOWARDS THOSE *LIGHTS*---

...AS A *MOTH* IS DRAWN TO *FLAME!*

THEY GROW BRIGHTER.. *BRIGHTER*..! THE GLARE IS *UNBEARABLE*... INTOLERABLE...

I'M IN THE GRIP OF A FORCE SO *ALL-CONSUMING* ---SO TOTALLY *ALIEN*---THAT---

ARHHHH!

28

YOUR BODY HAS BEEN *COMPLETELY* ENCASED IN A LIFE-PRESERVING *SILVERY SUBSTANCE* OF MY OWN CREATION!

A SUBSTANCE WHICH WILL SHIELD YOU FROM *HEAT*...FROM *COLD*...AND FROM LACK OF *OXYGEN*!

FROM THIS MOMENT FORTH---NEITHER THE FRIGID, MARROW-CHILLING EMPTINESS OF AIRLESS *SPACE*, NOR THE ALL-CONSUMING INFERNO OF THE HOTTEST *SUN* CAN CAUSE YOU HARM!

AND NOW...TO *TRANSPORT* YOU THRU THE ENDLESS COSMOS.

I SHALL PROVIDE THE *PERFECT* VEHICLE!

AN INDESTRUCTIBLE FLYING *BOARD*...

YOURS TO CONTROL...WITH BUT A SINGLE *THOUGHT*!

NOW, AND *FOREVERMORE*... YOU ARE MY *HERALD*!

NOW, AND *FOREVER-MORE*...YOU ARE TRULY...THE *SILVER SURFER*!

GO THEN...FOR THE LIMITLESS REACHES OF SPACE ARE *YOURS*!

GO... AND FIND ME A *WORLD*... TO ASSUAGE MY GNAWING *HUNGER*!

34

THIS IS WHAT I'VE *DREAMED* OF... THIS IS WHAT I'VE EVER *LONGED* FOR!

A LIFETIME OF ENDLESS *ADVENTURE* BECKONING BEFORE ME!

THERE MUST BE *NO REGRETS*... NO THOUGHTS OF *TURNING BACK!*

WORLDS WITHOUT *LIMIT* NOW AWAIT MY COMING!

AND I SHALL BE *TRUE* TO MY TRUST... FOR AS LONG AS I *LIVE!*

BUT, BEFORE I BEGIN THE *LONGEST JOURNEY* ANY MORTAL HAS EVER KNOWN---

THERE IS *ONE* TO WHOM I MUST BID *FAREWELL!*

EVER IN MY HEART WILL THERE BE A *LONGING*... FOR THE LOVELY *SHALLA BAL!*

DO NOT BE *ALARMED!*

I AM HIM WHO WAS... *NORRIN RADD!*

THEN...IT'S *TRUE!* YOU *REACHED* THE FLYING GLOBE! BUT, WHAT HAS *HAPPENED?* WHAT HAVE THEY *DONE* TO YOU?

MY FATE IS OF LITTLE CONSEQUENCE!

BUT LET NOT THE *SPIRIT* OF OUR ANCESTORS BE LOST A SECOND TIME! LET NOT OUR PEOPLE GROW SOFT AND INDOLENT!

SUFFICE IT TO SAY...THIS PLANET SHALL *NOT* PERISH!

HE WHO COMMANDS THE *GLOBE* WILL SOON *DEPART..* AND *ZENNA-LA* SHALL RISE AGAIN!

YOU... SOUND AS THOUGH..

YOU WILL NO LONGER ...BE AMONG US!

35

THEN, THE MOST FATEFUL MOMENT OF *ALL*...THE DISCOVERY OF THE PLANET *EARTH*...!

AT *LAST*! A WORLD TO NOURISH MY *MASTER*!

BUT, THERE IS *LIFE BELOW*! AND *YET*...

GALACTUS HAS JOURNEYED *FAR*... AND HIS *HUNGER* KNOWS NO BOUNDS!

IT WAS *HERE*...UPON THIS TORTURED WORLD...THAT I FIRST *DEFIED* HIM WHO HAD GIVEN ME MY *POWER*! FOR THOSE WHO DWELLED UPON THE *EARTH* HAD A SPECIAL SORT OF *GLORY*...*

STAY *BACK*, HERALD. THESE CREATURES ARE OF NO CONSEQUENCE TO *GALACTUS*!!

NO, *MASTER*-- *NO*!

YOU CANNOT DESTROY THE ENTIRE *HUMAN* RACE!

THEY ARE AS DESERVING OF LIFE AS *YOU*...OR *I*!

*...AS DID *FANTASTIC FOUR #50*, FROM WHENCE THIS STERLING SEQUENCE HATH BEEN TAKEN!--STOICAL STAN.

NEVER BEFORE HAD I DARED TO CHALLENGE *GALACTUS*! AND SO, IT *BEGAN*...!

NO MATTER *WHAT* MY FATE, I FACE IT WITHOUT QUALM!

FOR I HAVE LEARNED FROM THE *HUMANS* HOW GLORIOUS IT CAN BE TO HAVE A CAUSE WORTH *DYING* FOR!

OF ALL WHO LIVE, I HAVE CHERISHED *YOU* THE MOST!

BUT NOW, BY *MY* HAND---THE SILVER SURFER MUST *PERISH*!

NO! GALACTUS! IT IS *YOU* WHO WILL PERISH! FOR WE HAVE FOUND THE *WEAPON* AT LAST!

THE *ULTIMATE NULLIFIER*!! IN THE HANDS OF A *HUMAN*!

YOU HOLD THE MEANS TO DESTROY A *GALAXY*...TO LAY WASTE TO A *UNIVERSE*!*

* IF YOU *MISSED* F.F. #50, YOU'LL HAVE TO TAKE OUR *WORD* FOR ALL THIS! IT'S TOO *INVOLVED* TO EXPLAIN RIGHT HERE! --SQUEAMISH STAN.

37.

FOR THE *FIRST* TIME...SINCE THE DAWN OF *MEMORY*...MY WILL HAS BEEN *THWARTED!*

BUT, I BEAR *NO MALICE!* EMOTION IS FOR *LESSER BEINGS!*

YET, THERE IS *ONE* THING THAT MUST BE DONE..!

SINCE YOU SHALL BE HERALD TO GALACTUS *NO LONGER...*

I *REMOVE* YOUR SPACE-TIME POWERS!

HENCEFORTH THE *SILVER SURFER* SHALL ROAM THE GALAXIES *NO MORE!*

NOW HERE I STAND *ALONE AND FORE-SAKEN* UPON THIS HOSTILE WORLD!

I, WHO HAVE CRESTED THE WAVES OF *INFINITY*.. EXILED FOREVER UPON THIS LONELY SPHERE...

BUT, *TIME* IS LONG AND *FATE* IS FICKLE...

MY *DESTINY* STILL LIES *BEFORE* ME... AND WHERE IT BECKONS.. *THERE* SHALL SOAR THE *SILVER SURFER!*

NEXT ISSUE: WHEN LANDS THE SAUCER!

EPILOGUE

Well, we have to end somewhere. And, let's face it, The Silver Surfer's a pretty tough act to follow.

But even as we start folding our tents and wiping the inkwells dry, we sense that this is naught but a brief hiatus, a momentary pause in the never-ending march of Marvel mythos.

The years following the origin tales you've just read have brought many other new and dynamic features from the Bullpen to you. And the months which still lie ahead will see many more star-studded sagas sensationally spring to life on the pages of Marvel Comics.

As the days drift by, you'll discover the names of new artists, new writers, new editors and art directors being added to the world-famous roster of Marvel greats. And yet, the more things change, the more they remain the same. The same thrills, the same color, the same action and excitement, fantasy and imagination that have captivated you in the past will do so again in the future. Our world is the world of make-believe—and so long as men can think, so long as men can extrapolate, so long as men can fantasize, the rich and rewarding lode of Marvel legends will never ever die.

Excelsior!